KU-000-901

Maria Edgeworth

LETTERS FOR
LITERARY LADIES

to which is added

AN ESSAY ON THE NOBLE SCIENCE
OF SELF-JUSTIFICATION

(1795)

EVERYMAN

J. M. DENT · LONDON
CHARLES E. TUTTLE
VERMONT

Introduction and other critical apparatus
© J. M. Dent 1993

First published in Everyman by J. M. Dent 1993

Typeset at The Spartan Press Ltd.,
Lymington, Hants.

Printed in Great Britain by
The Guernsey Press Co. Ltd.,
Guernsey, C.I.

for
J. M. Dent
Orion Publishing Group
Orion House
5 Upper St Martin's Lane, London WC2H 9EA

and
Charles E. Tuttle Co. Inc.
28 South Main Street, Rutland, Vermont
05701 USA

British Library Cataloguing-in-Publication Data
is available upon request.

ISBN 0 460 87250 8

CONTENTS

NOTE ON THE AUTHOR AND EDITOR

Maria Edgeworth wrote with ease and insight of life both in England and Ireland, influenced perhaps by the early years she spent in Oxfordshire, Derby, Longford, and London. She was born in 1768 in her mother's family home, Black Bourton in Oxfordshire. In 1782 the family finally settled in Edgeworthstown, Co. Longford, Ireland, where her father Richard Lovell was determined to succeed as an improving landlord. He found his eldest daughter shared his ambition, and he set about educating her in political economy, agriculture and the practical management of an estate. Maria was, however, forbidden to read novels, on the advice of her father's friend, Thomas Day. The ban soon lapsed, and by the time Day died, in 1789, Maria had begun to pen her own stories. *Letters for Literary Ladies, to which is added an Essay on the Noble Science of Self-Justification* (1795) is her first published work. Much of her early work was written either in direct or close collaboration with her father, most notably *Practical Education* (1798) and the *Essay on Irish Bulls* (1802). She seems to have respected her father's opinion above all others, although *Castle Rackrent* (1800), and *Belinda* (1801) show less of his influence than critics sometimes like to think. She then published some stories for children, which exemplify many of her theories on education. Her Irish tales include *The Absentee* (1812), *Ormond* (1817), and *Ennui* (1809). *Leonora* (1806) and *Patronage* (1814) are rational romances set in Britain and, like *Belinda*, they elevate the role of the domestic woman. It is *Helen* (1834), the last novel, which asserted most strongly the author's continuing commitment to female education. Maria Edgeworth died in 1849, by which time her novels were already suffering from the vagaries of literary fashion. Today, however, her explorations of female education are regarded as lucid challenges to eighteenth-century theories of genre, gender, and the proper place of the woman writer.

Claire Connolly is a Lecturer in English Literature in the School of English Studies, University of Wales, College of Cardiff. She is completing a doctoral thesis on fictions of colonial history in the novels of Maria Edgeworth and Lady Morgan.

CHRONOLOGY

Year	Age	Key Events
1768		*1 January* Maria Edgeworth born in Black Bourton, Oxfordshire
1771		
1773	5	*March* Anna Maria Elers, ME's mother, dies; *July* her father Richard Lovell Edgeworth marries Honora Sneyd; the family moves to Edgeworthstown
1775	7	ME sent away to school in Derby
1776		
1777	9	The family moves back to England; RLE becomes closely involved with the Lunar circle, including Thomas Day, James Keir, Josiah Wedgwood, and Erasmus Darwin
1778		
1780	12	*April* Honora Sneyd dies; *December* RLE marries Elizabeth Sneyd, Honora's sister
1781	13	ME moves to a new school in London; she goes to stay with Thomas Day
1782	14	The whole family move back to Edgeworthstown

Year	Literary Context	Historical Events
1768		Octennial Act (Irish parliament's life limited to eight years)
1771	Henry Mackenzie, *The Man of Feeling*	
1773	Oliver Goldsmith, *She Stoops to Conquer*; Chesterfield dies	Boston tea party
1775	Jane Austen born	Battles of Lexington, Concord and Bunker Hill in the USA
1776	Adam Smith, *Wealth of Nations*; Jeremy Bentham, *A Fragment on Government; or, a Comment on the Commentaries*; Edward Gibbon, *Decline and Fall of the Roman Empire* (–1788); Charles Burney, *History of Music*; David Hume born	American Declaration of Independence
1777	Henry Mackenzie, *Julia de Roubigné*	American Congress adopts Confederation Articles of perpetual Union of United States
1778	Fanny Burney, *Evelina*; Richard Brinsley Sheridan, *The School for Scandal*; Jean Jacques Rousseau dies	Catholic Relief Act grants rights of leasing and inheritance
1780	Arthur Young, *Tour in Ireland*; Immanuel Kant, *Critique of Pure Reason*	Act opening colonial trade to Irish goods
1781	Jean Jacques Rousseau, *Confessions*	Cornwallis capitulates to American forces at Yorktown
1782	Fanny Burney, *Cecilia*; Dugald Stewart, *Elements of the Philosophy of the Human Mind*	Ireland achieves legislative independence

1783	Thomas Day, *Sandford and Merton* (–1789); Jean d'Alembert dies	Peace of Versailles agreed between Britain, France, Spain, and USA; Britain officially recognizes USA
1785	Thomas de Quincey born	Royal Irish Academy founded; steam engine with rotary motion installed by Matthew Boulton and James Watt in Nottingham-shire
1788		The Regency crisis; the trial of Warren Hastings begins
1789	William Blake, *Songs of Innocence*	French Revolution
1790	Edmund Burke, *Reflections on the Revolution in France*; Adam Smith dies	
1791	Elizabeth Inchbald, *A Simple Story*; Thomas Paine, *The Rights of Man, I*	Theobald Wolfe Tone founds the Society of United Irish-men
1792	Mary Wollstonecraft, *A Vindication of the Rights of Woman*; Thomas Paine, *The Rights of Man, II*	Catholic Relief Act allows Catholics to practise law
1793		Further Relief Act grants Catholics parliamentary franchise and some civil and military rights
1795	Samuel Taylor Coleridge, *Conciones ad Populum*; John Keats born	Act providing for establishment of Catholic seminary, opened as Royal College of St Patrick at Maynooth; the Directory in France; Napoleon Bonaparte made commander of the army; Mungo Park explores the course of the River Niger
1796	Fanny Burney, *Camilla*	Insurrection Act in Ireland; Habeas Corpus suspended
1797	Samuel Coleridge, *Kubla Khan*; Edmund Burke dies; Mary Wollstonecraft dies	Irish Whigs invite the Prince of Wales to become Lord Lieutenant of Ireland
1798	Mary Hays, *Memoirs of Emma Courtney; An Appeal to the Men of Great Britain on Behalf of the Women*	Rebellion in Wexford defeated; General Humbert's French forces land in Co. Mayo, move almost as far as Co. Longford before defeat

1800	32	*Castle Rackrent, an Hibernian Tale*
1801	33	*Harry and Lucy*, parts I and II; *Rosamond*, parts I–III; *Frank*, parts I–IV; *Moral Tales for Young People*, 5 vols; *Belinda*, 3 vols
1802	34	With RLE, *Essay on Irish Bulls*; ME and RLE visit Brussels and Paris; Chevalier Edelcrantz proposes marriage to ME and is refused
1803	35	Forced to leave Paris, as Napoleonic Wars resume; return to England
1804	36	*Popular Tales*, 3 vols
1805	37	*The Modern Griselda, a tale*
1806	38	*Leonora*, 2 vols
1809	41	With RLE, *Essays on Professional Education*; also *Tales of Fashionable Life*, vols I–III (*Ennui, Almeria, Madame de Fleury, The Dun, Manoeuvring*)
1812	44	*Tales of Fashionable Life*, vols IV–VI (*Vivian, Emilie de Coulanges, The Absentee*)
1813	45	Visit to London, where ME meets Byron and Humphry Davy
1814	46	*Patronage*, 4 vols; *Continuation of Early Lessons*, 2 vols; reads *Waverly*; begins correspondence with Walter Scott
1817	49	*Harrington, a tale;* and *Ormond, a tale*, 3 vols; RLE dies
1819	51	Travels to London

1800	Humphry Davy, *Researches, Chemical and Philosophical, Chiefly Concerning Nitrous Oxide*; Thomas Babington Macaulay born	Act of Union passed in Irish parliament
1801	Robert Southey, *Thalaba the Destroyer*	Union takes effect; Pitt resigns over royal veto on Catholic emancipation
1802	Mme de Staël, *Delphine*	Britain signs Peace of Amiens with France
1803	Erasmus Darwin, *Temple of Nature*	Failed rising of Robert Emmet
1804	Amelia Opie, *Adeline Mowbray*	Napoleon becomes Emperor
1805	Walter Scott, *The Lay of the Last Minstrel*	Battles of Trafalgar and Austerlitz
1806	Sydney Owenson (Lady Morgan), *The Wild Irish Girl*	Pitt dies; "Ministry of all the Talents", with Grenvile as PM
1809	*Quarterly Review* founded by Scott and others; Walter Scott, *Marmion*; Johann Wolfgang von Goethe, *The Elective Affinities*	Napoleon imprisons Pope Pius VII
1812	Lord Byron, *Childe Harold's Pilgrimage*; Percy Bysshe Shelley, *Address to the Irish People*; Charles Dickens born	War with USA; Napoleon invades Russia
1813	Jane Austen, *Pride and Prejudice*;	Wellington defeats the French at Vittoria
1814	Walter Scott, *Waverly*; Lady Morgan, *O'Donnel*	Fall of Paris; Napoleon abdicates
1817	Thomas Moore, *Lallah Rookh*; David Ricardo, *Principles of Political Economy and Taxation*; Jane Austen dies	Habeas Corpus suspended in Britain
1819	Walter Scott, *Tales of My Landlord*; George Eliot born	Peterloo Massacre

1820	52	*Memoirs of Richard Lovell Edgeworth, Begun by himself and concluded by his daughter*
1821	53	*Rosamond: a sequel to Early Lessons*, 2 vols
1822	54	*Frank: a sequel to Frank in Early Lessons*, 3 vols
1823	55	Goes to Edinburgh; visits Scott in Abbotsford
1825	57	*Harry and Lucy Concluded: being the last part of Early Lessons*, 4 vols
1826	58	Takes over management of the estate from her brother, Lovell
1827		
1830		
1833	65	Visits Connemara
1834	66	*Helen, a tale*, 3 vols
1837		
1840		
1843		
1845		
1846		
1847		
1848	80	*Orlandino*
1849	81	ME dies

1820	Walter Scott, *Ivanhoe*; Percy Bysshe Shelley, *Prometheus Unbound*; Thomas Malthus, *Principles of Political Economy*	Accession of George VI
1821	Thomas de Quincey, *Confessions of an English Opium Eater*; Walter Scott, *Kenilworth*; Keats dies	Death of Napoleon
1822	John Galt, *The Provost*; Shelley dies	Irish Constabulary Act
1823	Walter Scott, *Quentin Durward*; Mary Shelley, *Valperga*	Catholic Association founded; war between France and Spain
1825	Thomas Crofton Croker, *Fairy Legends and Traditions of the South of Ireland*; James Stuart Mill, *Essays on Government*; Anna Laetitia Barbauld dies	Lords reject Catholic Emancipation Bill
1826	Benjamin Disraeli, *Vivian Grey*; Mary Shelley, *The Last Man*	
1827	Lady Morgan, *The O'Briens and the O'Flahertys*	
1830		Accession of William IV
1833	Thomas Carlyle, *Sartor Resartus*	British Factory Act passed
1834	Honoré de Balzac, *La Recherche de l'Absolu*	O'Connell introduces debate on Repeal of Union; slavery abolished in the British Empire
1837		Accession of Victoria
1840		Repeal Association founded
1843		First "monster" Repeal meeting
1845		Irish famine begins
1846		Repeal of the Corn Laws
1847		Death of Daniel O'Connell
1848		First publication of Fenian journal, *United Irishman*; Fenian rebellion put down

INTRODUCTION

Maria Edgeworth was brought up to believe that a sound education, not gender, was the ultimate measure of ability. This hardly equipped her to deal with eighteenth-century notions of femininity, which were based on women's exclusion from the public spheres of power and knowledge. *Letters for Literary Ladies*, Maria Edgeworth's first published work, negotiates the gap between her faith in the Enlightenment promise of progress, and her growing awareness of Enlightenment fear and distrust of women.

I

Maria Edgeworth's own education began unremarkably enough. Born in Oxfordshire, she spent her first years being either mildly indulged or generally ignored. In 1773, however, Anna Maria Elers, Maria's mother, died, and with her went her daughter's easy going existence. Her father, Richard Lovell Edgeworth, swiftly remarried and moved to Edgeworthstown in Ireland. His new wife was the formidable Honora Sneyd, whom the young Maria feared and respected. Honora Sneyd and her new husband shared strong convictions on the education of children; and when they sent Maria away to school in Derby, they wrote her regular letters, as part of her training. These letters are full of observations on her progress, and explanations of their future plans for her development. By the time Maria was ten, her father was already writing to her, looking forward to when she "might become a very excellent, & an highly improved woman". Her many siblings were subjected to similar pressures

– when she was younger still, she had witnessed her brother, Richard, being educated according to Jean Jacques Rousseau's theories of natural learning. In *Emile* (1762), Rousseau sets out principles of natural reason, and encourages parents to teach their sons by experience and explanation. In fact, the young Richard actually learned far more independence of thought than his father thought proper, with the result that Richard Lovell Edgeworth abandoned Rousseauistic theories altogether.

In 1777, Richard Lovell Edgeworth and Honora Sneyd moved back to England, this time to Hertfordshire. Living in Ireland had proved a financial disaster, but Edgeworth was also anxious to rediscover the intellectual stimulation he felt was lacking in Edgeworthstown. In 1766 he had met the scientist Erasmus Darwin, who had, in turn, introduced him to Midland industrialists Matthew Boulton and Dr William Small. All three were core members of what had just been named the "Lunar" society. As a group, their interests were often diverse, but they were jointly committed to industrial progress through enlightened scientific methods. Mechanization, its members felt, would bring progress and prosperity. Amongst its other members were Josiah Wedgwood, the founder of the famous pottery firm, and James Keir, an industrial chemist. Richard Lovell Edgeworth's enthusiasm for mechanics turned his attention from education for a while, although he was later to bring Lunar faith in progress and reform to his pedagogical practice. In 1780, Honora Sneyd died, bequeathing as a final wish her hope that her husband might marry her sister. Despite the disapproval of the Sneyd family, Edgeworth married Elizabeth Sneyd eight months later, in December 1780. Maria was then moved to another school, this time to a more fashionable establishment in London. It was during her time at Mrs Devis's Academy for Young Ladies that the ideas for *Letters for Literary Ladies* began to take shape.

Maria Edgeworth's closest friend at school was her classmate, Fanny Robinson. They remained correspondents for a number of years, but when Fanny left school she returned to the fashionable world of which Edgeworth knew nothing. Their letters seem to be full of misapprehensions and confusion: Fanny's letters describe balls and dresses, while Maria gravely considers the morals of the Irish peasantry or the ethics of novel-reading. When she went to stay with the newly established Mrs (Robinson) Hoare in London in 1792, she returned aghast at society life:

> The more I see of others, the more I like the character, manners & way of life of my own family. She was exceedingly kind to me, and I spent most of my time with her as I liked; I say most because a good deal of it was spent in company where I heard of nothing but Chariots and Horses [,] Curricles and Tandems. Oh, to what contempt I exposed myself in a luckless hour by asking what a Tandem was!

As Marilyn Butler has pointed out,[1] this correspondence became the basis for the letters between Julia and Caroline in *Letters for Literary Ladies*. The "Letters" convert the episode into a fictional victory for "the way of life" of the Edgeworths, excluding the dangerous world of fashion and "superficial knowledge".

Maria Edgeworth had few other friends at school, but she did find rather unlikely companionship in the home of one of her father's friends. Thomas Day was an old friend of her father's who lived in Surrey. He visited Maria at school, and she spent some of her holidays with him and his wife. This must have pleased Richard Lovell Edgeworth, who admired and respected Day's commitment to education. Day had, in fact, been responsible for Edgeworth's Rousseauistic experiments with his son. However, Edgeworth had turned away from Rousseau towards the more enlightened views of his Lunar friends, whereas Day remained a committed believer. In particular, he continued to endorse Rousseau's views on the education of women. At the end of *Emile*, the hero encounters a young woman brought up in perfect seclusion. Sophie is the ideal woman whom Emile marries. Her education, however, while also free of conventional pedagogical authority, is a schooling in submission. As Day had no children of his own on whom to experiment, he decided to educate a wife after Rousseau's method.[2] Predictably, this experiment failed, but it did not shake Day's faith in the efficacy of Rousseau's theories of female education. He was horrified that his friend was encouraging the young Maria to read philosophy and politics. His outrage was even greater when Richard Lovell Edgeworth told him he had also begun to encourage his daughter to write. Edgeworth had, in fact, asked his daughter to begin a translation of Madame de Genlis' *Adèle et Théodore: ou, lettres sur l'education*. *Adelaide and Theodore* was, in fact, never published as another translation made it to the shelves first. This delighted Day (himself an author of children's fiction[3]). He wrote at once to Richard Lovell Edgeworth, congratulating him on saving his daughter from the despicable world of female authorship. Maria based the first two letters in *Letters for Literary Ladies* on this exchange.

The Edgeworths all returned to Ireland in 1782, which signalled an end to Maria's formal schooling, and the beginning of her literary collaboration with her father. After her disappointment with the translation, she turned her attention to drama for a short spell. Marilyn Butler locates a confident, "natural" tone emerging in her work from 1786 onwards, and during the early 1790s she began composing more and more simple children's stories in this tone.[4] Day's death in 1789 removed the ban on publishing, and most of these early stories are collected in *The Parent's Assistant*, published in 1795. Maria Edgeworth's distinctive fictional voice begins to emerge here: *Simple Susan*, *Lazy Lawrence* and, most of all, the "Rosamond" stories capture much of the openness and curiosity of childhood, and only rarely make style subject to a moral.

In 1795, Maria Edgeworth also published *Letters for Literary Ladies, to which is added an Essay on the Noble Science of Self-Justification*. From then until 1798, she worked with her father on completing a work he had originally intended to write with his second wife, Honora Sneyd. It was to be an educational treatise aimed at "enlightened parents" anxious for guidance. *Practical Education* was published in 1798, the fruit of several years' reading and discussion. It is a learned discussion of "practical" means of bringing up children to think for themselves. It rejects the notion of education as a series of "accomplishments" to be acquired, and insists that children should learn the basic principle of reason, from which all else will follow. Maria Edgeworth's speculative confidence derived from her continuing education, which grew increasingly unconventional. Once she had her father's full attention in Edgeworthstown, she absorbed a wide range of contemporary intellectual and political opinions, mostly through her father and his friends. Her political ideology was intially drawn from her voracious reading: she was familiar with the writings of Edmund Burke, Adam Smith, Adam Ferguson, and Jeremy Bentham. She distilled her broad reading into a social philosophy committed above all to the advancement of society through education. Alongside this basically conservative outlook, however, went a firm intellectual resolution. She is rarely overawed by established authority, and always reserves the right to criticize existing institutions: her political philosophy illustrates clearly Jeremy Bentham's "motto of a good citizen": "To obey punctually; to censure freely".[5] This spirit of social inquiry is clear in *Practical Education* (1798), where she declares that a young woman must be educated in reason as well as obedience:

> Her knowledge must be various, and her powers of reasoning unawed by authority; yet she must habitually feel the nice sense of propriety, which is alone the guard and charm of every feminine virtue.[6]

This combination of intelligence and coy propriety is exactly what makes her next published work such a curious text. *Castle Rackrent; an Hibernian Tale* (1800) is marked by an anarchic textual and political energy. It flatters, challenges and frustrates its readers. It stands in marked contrast to her next publication, *Moral Tales*, a collection of stories for older children, which appeared in 1801. Among the most entertaining of these stories is "Angelina", a clever satire on popular literary trends, from the novel of ideas, the literature of sensibility, to picturesque description. Maria Edgeworth's ideas about literature find a more sustained expression in her major publication of that year,

Belinda. The novel was written between May 1800 and the spring of 1801, just after Maria had returned from a short trip to England with her father and his new wife, Frances Beaufort. While Richard Lovell Edgeworth was away, his daughter's reading matter consisted largely of novels, although early in her career they had been forbidden to her by her father, who was influenced by Thomas Day's opinions on the subject. (Day was as opposed to women reading novels as he was to their writing them.) Despite *Belinda*'s standard disclaimer, that it should not be read merely as a work of fiction, "the author not wishing to acknowledge a Novel",[7] it heralded a new era in its author's popularity. Its heroine is a prototype of the domestic woman who appears in many of Maria Edgeworth's novels, but the novel also releases some forbidden voices. Alongside the model domestic woman, Mrs Percival, the novel features a furious female philosopher, Harriet Freke, and the engaging if corrupt Lady Delacour. They do battle for Belinda's soul, and although Mrs Percival's influence triumphs, somehow the novel's conclusion is never quite convincing. In *The Modern Griselda* (1805), she is on altogether surer ground, probably because the tale's generic politics, those of the Enlightenment "conte", threaten none of the "folly, error and vice" disseminated by the novel form.[8] *Leonora* (1806) is less cautious, and warily finds its way into the murky waters of French and German fiction and morals, criticizing their pernicious effect on English lives. *Leonora* is, however, less successful than *Belinda* in holding its philosophic principles intact, for the reader does glimpse something like a real threat to English domestic order.

Maria Edgeworth's own experience was not, of course, confined to Edgeworthstown, nor indeed to London. In 1802 she travelled with her father and the family through the industrial Midlands, on to London, and from there to Flanders, Bruges and Paris. It was in Paris in 1803 that she received her famous proposal of marriage from a Swedish diplomat, the Chevalier Edelcrantz. She refused him and later that year returned to Edgeworthstown via Edinburgh. Maria Edgeworth travelled to Britain and to Europe again, but made her home in Edgeworthstown, where she remained until her death in 1849.

II

Despite Maria Edgeworth's formidable literary and philosophical training, she never took authorship for granted. Even as a well-known writer, she continued to denigrate her role and to fight shy of the literary world. *Letters for Literary Ladies* goes some way towards illuminating the nature of this unease. Eighteenth-century definitions of literary authority rested on a number of key cultural antagonisms. The role of the writer was defined and determined by existing systems of generic, sexual and biological difference. In this system, philosophy was privileged over fiction, just as reasonable speech was superior to emotional outbursts. The discourse of reason found its proper place in the calm, abstract speculations of philosophy, which addressed and interpellated "man", or more correctly, men, the rational agents of knowledge. Common-sense speculations on this shared knowledge demanded a plain style, uncontaminated by the ambiguities of language. Yet to eschew language entirely was impossible, so its slipperiness remains a potential threat, skirting the edges of plain speech, disrupting the ordering of knowledge. Novels, on the other hand, revelled in the excess of words. They exploited ambiguity and indulged in emotion, just as women were accused of deceit, untrustworthiness and hysteria. These shifting cultural meanings are written into the history of *Letters for Literary Ladies*. Maria Edgeworth revised the second letter in favour of female education only three years after it was first published. In the Advertisement to the 1798 edition, she explained how the 1795 version was thought to undercut its own argument. But how could it not? It addresses its readers in the plain style revered by Enlightenment thinkers. It does not deign to offer any anecdote or example, but simply argues that it is only reasonable that women should be properly educated. It avoids the circularity of the first letter, and simply states its case as plain fact. But Edgeworth's critics were correct, for the argument has no real impact. Reasonable argument cannot exist independently of persuasion, conviction, and all the other rhetorical tricks that writers of novels understood. This perhaps explains Edgeworth's contradictory feelings towards fiction: she told Fanny Robinson that:

> Though I am as fond of Novels as you can be I am afraid they act on the constitution of the mind as Drams do on that of the body –

Yet she read and enjoyed novels, perhaps finding in them an outlet for what she later described as the "different feelings" which threatened to disrupt her rational speculations. In 1811, she wrote to Etienne Dumont, a Swiss utilitarian, describing how:

> A number of different feelings – many of them most trifling and foolish perhaps – . . . disturb my spirit of observation and unfit me for a *philosophical spectatress* in the world.

This rather clumsy noun hints at an almost unspoken understanding that the act of observation is a male role. Women (as well as children, members of other cultures, and the lower classes) are sometimes the objects of rational curiosity, but rarely assume the awkward title of *"spectatress"*. Late eighteenth-century writers could, of course, negotiate and challenge this system of differences, but its cultural authority was difficult to dislodge. We need only turn to Mary Wollstonecraft's *A Vindication of the Rights of Woman* (1792) to see the strains imposed on the female philosopher. In order to gain access to the public sphere of philosophy, she has to deny "feminine" excesses of language: "I shall disdainds to cull my phrases or polish my style", she declares, although her text is densely literary and almost novelistic. *Letters for Literary Ladies* also stands in an uneasy relationship to this system of differences; but whereas *A Vindication of the Rights of Woman* provoked its eighteenth-century audience by stepping into the public sphere, *Letters for Literary Ladies* enacts a more subtle transgression.

III

Although Maria Edgeworth's unconventional education never quite condemned her to the lonely fate predicted by the "Letter from a Gentleman to his Friend", it does make it difficult to place her as part of any discernible group or movement. If anything, her only apparent allegiances are to her father's peers, rather than her own. She did subscribe to Lunar principles, and aided and encouraged her father in his various mechanical schemes — the most notorious of which involved installing a telegraph system in Ireland. Yet somehow one feels her dutiful daughter's heart was never in this project. In the first edition of the letter in favour of female education, she makes a brave effort at applying this enthusiasm for scientific knowledge to her own concerns, when she argues that:

> a good cook is only an empirical chemist, and that the study of this science would produce a salutary reform in receipt books, and must improve the accomplishments of every lady who unites in her person the offices of housekeeper and wife.

This example does not recur in the second edition, however; an acknowledgement, perhaps, of the strain it puts on the argument. To note Edgeworth's troubled involvement in her father's projects is not, however, to argue, as Beth Kowaleski-Wallace does, that Maria Edgeworth was psychologically dependent on her father, and that:

> It should be of little wonder to us that she should repeatedly articulate a discourse not her own.[9]

This is to deny Edgeworth's own stake in the discourse of scientific rationalism. Rather, we can look at her redefinitions of that discourse. These cluster around Enlightenment notions of femininity. Female education is a central concern, and it is here, amongst the texts of other rational women writers, that Maria Edgeworth's writings find their literary constituency. The end of the century of Shaftesbury, Hume, and Richardson saw a female backlash against the illusory benefits to women of the cult of sensibility. In *Camilla* (1796), Fanny Burney laments the power of "wayward Sensibility", and Jane Austen's *Sense and Sensibility* (1811) was later to seek to demonstrate just how dangerous indulging in sensibility could be for women. Like Jane Austen, Edgeworth wholeheartedly ridiculed the cult of sensibility. As an admiring Helen Zimmern, one of Edgeworth's Victorian biographers, points out:

> She loved to expose the fashionable and mawkish doctrines thought fit for women.[10]

This perfectly summarizes "Letters of Julia and Caroline", which sets up a debate between a rational woman and her sentimental friend. Julia's first letter is followed by five letters from Caroline, all "quoting" from Julia's "other" letters, and paraphrasing their arguments. This is a disabling strategy, one which guarantees Caroline's ultimate moral victory, which she herself has already predicted.

The price of such certainty is exclusion. Julia's voice is heard only indirectly, as it threatens the fabric of Caroline's world. If women were allowed to rant, cry and moan, how could they ever stand on an equal footing with men? Such eruptions of feminine emotion threatened the smooth surface of Enlightenment discourse. Caroline is calm, rational and respected by her husband, and thus guaranteed domestic harmony. Yet she pays the price of her felicity, for Caroline is one in a long series of Edgeworthian heroines who must sacrifice pleasure to principle. It is curious that it is in the essay, the genre most intimately associated with rational argument and masculine logic, that we encounter the text's only indulgence in emotion. The "Essay on the Noble Science of Self-Justification" might be the response of a more able Julia. It signifies the return of repressed emotion, passion and pleasure, as it assumes an uncompromisingly "feminine" voice. This is only possible because of the text's redefinition of femininity. But it conducts most of its reasonable, philosophic argument via that most unstable of genres, the letter form. Epistolary fiction marks out a new space for itself, one somewhere between the public and the private, the logical and the spontaneous. *Letters for Literary Ladies* makes the same gesture in the name of what might have been called *epistolary philosophy*.

I would gratefully like to acknowledge the help and advice of Robin Moffet, Stephen Copley and David Skilton.

CLAIRE CONNOLLY

Cardiff, 1993

1. Letter from Maria Edgeworth to her aunt, Mrs Ruxton, 6 November 1762; Marilyn Butler, *Maria Edgeworth: A Literary Biography*, Oxford, 1972, pp.108, 173.

2. Maria Edgeworth had a low opinion of this project, and demonstrated the fallacies of such a plan in a subplot of *Belinda* (1801).

3. Thomas Day was most famous for his *Sandford and Merton*, 1783–9. However, the Edgeworths never quite approved of his adherence to Rousseau's theories of education.

4. Butler, pp.154–5.

5. Jeremy Bentham, *A Fragment on Government; or, A Comment on the Commentaries*, London, 1823, p.399.

6. Richard Lovell Edgeworth and Maria Edgeworth, *Practical Education*, London, 1798, p.534.

7. Maria Edgeworth, Advertisement to *Belinda*, 1801, p.2. This is the "ungenerous and impolitic custom" of late eighteenth-century women writers, which Jane Austen ridicules in *Northanger Abbey* (1818).

8. Advertisement, p.2.

9. Beth Kowaleski-Wallace, "Milton's Daughters: The Education of Eighteenth-Century Women Writers", *Feminist Studies*, 12, 2, Summer 1986, p.283.

10. Helen Zimmern, *Maria Edgeworth: Eminent Women Series*, London 1883, p.131.

NOTE ON THE TEXT

Letters for Literary Ladies was first published in 1795. A second, revised edition appeared in 1798. The only changes were to the second letter, the "Answer to the preceding letter", which is from the gentleman arguing in favour of female education. Maria Edgeworth changed very little of the substance of the argument, but added many more examples to strengthen the case. In the Advertisement to the second edition, she explained:

> In the first edition, the Second Letter upon the advantages of cultivating the female understanding, was thought to weaken the cause it was intended to support. – That letter has been written over again; no pains have been spared to improve it, and to assert more strongly the female right to literature.

In order to do justice to Maria Edgeworth's pains, as well as to her political agenda, the text reproduced here is that of the second edition.

LETTER FROM A GENTLEMAN TO HIS FRIEND, UPON THE BIRTH OF A DAUGHTER

I congratulate you, my dear sir, upon the birth of your daughter; and I wish that some of the fairies of ancient times were at hand to endow the damsel with health, wealth, wit, and beauty. Wit? — I should make a long pause before I accepted of this gift for a daughter – you would make none.

As I know it to be your opinion that it is in the power of education, more certainly than it was ever believed to be in the power of fairies, to bestow all mental gifts; and as I have heard you say that education should begin as early as possible, I am in haste to offer you my sentiments, lest my advice should come too late.

Your general ideas of the habits and virtues essential to the perfection of the female character nearly agree with mine; but we differ materially as to the cultivation which it is necessary or expedient to bestow upon the understandings of women. You are a champion for the rights of woman, and insist upon the equality of the sexes: but since the days of chivalry are past, and since modern gallantry permits men to speak, at least to one another, in less sublime language of the fair; I may confess to you that I see neither from experience nor analogy much reason to believe that, in the human species alone, there are no marks of inferiority in the female: – curious and admirable exceptions there may be, but many such have not fallen within my observation. I cannot say that I have been much enraptured, either on a first view or on a closer inspection, with female prodigies. Prodigies are scarcely less offensive to my taste than monsters: humanity makes us refrain from expressing disgust at the awkward shame of the one, whilst the intemperate vanity of the other justly provokes ridicule and indignation. I have always observed in the understandings of women who have been too much cultivated, some disproportion between the different faculties of their minds. One power of the mind undoubtedly may be cultivated at the expense of the rest; as we see that one muscle or limb may acquire excessive strength, and an unnatural size, at the expense of the health of the whole body: I cannot think this desirable, either for the individual or for society. – The unfortunate people in certain mountains of Switzerland are, some of them, proud of the excrescence by which they are deformed. I have seen women vain of exhibiting mental deformities, which to me appeared no less disgusting.[1] In the course of my life it has never been my good fortune to meet with a female whose mind, in strength, just proportion, and activity, I could compare to that of a sensible man.

Allowing, however, that women are equal to our sex in natural abilities; from their situation in society, from their domestic duties, their taste for dissipation, their love of romance, poetry, and all the lighter parts of literature, their time must be so fully occupied, that they could never have leisure for, even supposing that they were capable of, that severe application to which our sex submit. – Between persons of equal genius and equal industry, time becomes the only measure of their acquirements. — Now calculate the time which is wasted by the fair sex, and tell me how much the start of us they ought to have in the beginning of the race, if they are to reach the goal before us? – It is not possible that women should ever be our equals in knowledge, unless you assert that they are far our superiors in natural capacity. – Not only time but opportunity must be wanting to complete female studies: – we mix with the world without restraint, we converse freely with all classes of people, with men of wit, of science, of learning, with the artist, the mechanic, the labourer; every scene of life is open to our view; every assistance that foreign or domestic ingenuity can invent, to encourage literary studies, is ours almost exclusively. From academies, colleges, public libraries, private associations of literary men, women are excluded, if not by law, at least by custom, which cannot easily be conquered. — Whenever women appear, even when we seem to admit them as our equals in understanding, every thing assumes a different form; our politeness, delicacy, habits towards the sex, forbid us to argue or to converse with them as we do with one another: — we see things as they are; but women must always see things through a veil, or cease to be women. — With these insuperable difficulties in their education and in their passage through life, it seems impossible that their minds should ever acquire that vigour and *efficiency*, which accurate knowledge and various experience of life and manners can bestow.

Much attention has lately been paid to the education of the female sex; and you will say that we have been amply repaid for our care, — that ladies have lately exhibited such brilliant proofs of genius, as must dazzle and confound their critics. I do not ask for proofs of genius, I ask for solid proofs of utility. In which of the useful arts, in which of the exact sciences, have we been assisted by female sagacity or penetration? — I should be glad to see a list of discoveries, of inventions, of observations, evincing patient research, of truths established upon actual experiment, or deduced by just reasoning from previous principles: — if these, or any of these, can be presented by a female champion for her sex, I shall be the first to clear the way for her to the temple of Fame.[2]

I must not speak of my contemporaries, else candour might oblige me to allow that there are some few instances of great talents applied to useful purposes: — but, except these, what have been the literary productions of women! In poetry, plays, and romances, in the art of imposing upon the understanding by means of the imagination, they have excelled; — but to useful literature they have scarcely turned their thoughts. I have never heard of any female proficients in science — few have pretended to science till within these few years.

You will tell me, that in the most difficult and most extensive science of politics women have succeeded; — you will cite the names of some illustrious queens. I am inclined to think, with the Duke of Burgundy, that "queens who reigned well were governed by men, and kings who reigned ill were governed by women."[3]

The isolated examples of a few heroines cannot convince me that it is safe or expedient to trust the sex with power: – their power over themselves has regularly been found to diminish, in proportion as their power over others has been increased. I should not refer you to the scandalous chronicles of modern times, to volumes of private anecdotes, or to the abominable secret histories of courts, where female influence and female depravity are synonymous terms;[4] but I appeal to the open equitable page of history, to a body of evidence collected from the testimony of ages, for experiments tried upon the grandest scale of which nature admits, registered by various hands, without the possibility of collusion, and without a view to any particular system: – from these you must be convinced, that similar consequences have uniformly resulted from the same causes, in nations the most unlike, and at periods the most distant. Trace the history of female nature, from the court of Augustus to the court of Louis XIV, and tell me whether you can hesitate to acknowledge that the influence, the liberty, and the *power* of women have been constant concomitants of the moral and political decline of empires;[5] – I say the concomitants: where events are thus invariably connected, I might be justified in saying that they were *causes* – you would call them *effects*; but we need not dispute about the momentary precedence of evils, which are found to be inseparable companions: – they may be alternately cause and effect, – the reality of the connexion is established; it may be difficult to ascertain precisely its nature.

You will assert, that the fatal consequences which have resulted from our trusting the sex with liberty and power, have been originally occasioned by the subjection and ignorance in which they had previously been held, and of our subsequent folly and imprudence, in *throwing the reins of dominion into hands unprepared and uneducated to guide them.* I am at a loss to conceive any system of education that can properly prepare women for the exercise of power. Cultivate their understandings, "cleanse the visual orb with euphrasy and rue",[6] till they can with one comprehensive glance take in "one half at least of round eternity"; still you have no security that their reason will govern their conduct. The moral character seems, even amongst men of superior strength of mind, to have no certain dependence upon the reasoning faculty; – habit, prejudice, taste, example, and the different strength of various passions, form the moral character. We are impelled to action, frequently contrary to the belief of our sober reason; and we pursue what we could, in the hour of deliberation, demonstrate to be inconsistent with *that greatest possible share of happiness*, which it is the object of every rational creature to secure. We frequently "think with one species of enthusiasm, and act with another": and can we expect from women more consistency of conduct, if they are allowed the same liberty? — No one can feel, more strongly than you do, the necessity and the value of female integrity; no one can more clearly perceive how much in society depends upon the honour of women; and how much it is the interest of every individual, as well as of every state, to guard their virtue, and to preserve inviolate the purity of their manners. Allow me, then, to warn you of the danger of talking in loud strains to the sex, of the noble contempt of prejudice. You would look with horror at one who should go to sap the foundations of the building; beware then how you venture to tear away the ivy which clings to the walls, and braces the loose stones together.

I am by no means disposed to indulge in the fashionable ridicule of prejudice.[7] There is a sentimental, metaphysical argument, which, independently of all others, has lately been used, to prevail upon us to relinquish that superiority which strength of body in savage, and strength of mind in civilized nations, secure to man. We are told, that as women are reasonable creatures, they should be governed only by reason; and that we *disgrace* ourselves, and *enslave* them, when we instil even the most useful truths as prejudices. – Morality should, we are told, be founded upon demonstration, not upon sentiment; and we should not require human beings to submit to any laws or customs, without convincing their understandings of the universal utility of these political conventions. When are we to expect this conviction? We cannot expect it from childhood, scarcely from youth; but from the maturity of the understanding we are told that we may expect it with certainty. – And of what use can it then be to us? When the habits are fixed, when the character is decided, when the manners are formed, what can be done by the bare conviction of the understanding? What could we expect from that woman, whose moral education was to begin, at the moment when she was called upon to *act*; and who, without having imbibed in her early years any of the salutary prejudices of her sex, or without having been educated in the amiable acquiescence to well established maxims of female prudence, should boldly venture to conduct herself by the immediate conviction of her understanding? I care not for the names or titles of my guides; all that I shall inquire is, which is best acquainted with the road. Provided women be conducted quietly to their good, it is scarcely worth their while to dispute about the pompous metaphysical names, or precedency of their motives. Why should they deem it disgraceful to be induced to pursue their interest by what some philosophers are pleased to call *weak* motives? Is it not much less disgraceful to be peaceably governed by weak reasons, than to be incapable of being restrained by the strongest? The dignity of human nature, and the boasted free-will of rational agents, are high-sounding words, likely to impose upon the vanity of the fair sex, as well as upon the pride of ours; but if we analyze the ideas annexed to these terms, to what shall we reduce them? Reason in its highest perfection seems just to arrive at the certainty of instinct; and truth impressed upon the mind in early youth by the united voice of affection and authority, gives all the real advantages of the most investigating spirit of philosophy. If the result of the thought, experience, and sufferings of one race of beings is, (when inculcated upon the belief of the next,) to be stigmatized as prejudice, there is an end to all the benefits of history and of education. The mutual intercourse of individuals and of nations must be only for the traffic or amusement of the day. Every age must repeat the same experiments; every man and every nation must make the same mistakes, and suffer the same miseries, whilst the civilization and happiness of the world, if not retrograde in their course, must for ever be stationary.

Let us not then despise, or teach the other sex to despise, the traditional maxims of experience, or those early prepossessions, which may be termed prejudices, but which in reality serve as their moral instinct. I can see neither tyranny on our part, nor slavery on theirs, in this system of education. This sentimental or metaphysical appeal to our candour and generosity has then no real force; and every other argument for the *literary* and *philosophical* education of women, and for the extraordinary cultivation of their understandings, I have examined.

You probably imagine that, by the superior ingenuity and care you may bestow on your daughter's education, you shall make her an exception to general maxims; you shall give her all the blessings of a literary cultivation, and at the same time preserve her from all the follies, and faults, and evils, which have been found to attend the character of a literary lady.

Systems produce projects; and as projects in education are of all others the most hazardous, they should not be followed till after the most mature deliberation. Though it may be natural, is it wise for any man to expect extraordinary success, from his efforts or his precautions, beyond what has ever been the share of those who have had motives as strong for care and for exertion, and some of whom were possibly his equals in ability? Is it not incumbent upon you, as a parent and as a philosopher, to calculate accurately what you have to fear, as well as what you have to hope? You can at present, with a sober degree of interest, bear to hear me enumerate the evils, and ridicule the foibles, incident to literary ladies; but if your daughter were actually in this class, you would not think it friendly if I were to attack them. In this favourable moment, then, I beg you to hear me with temper; and as I touch upon every danger and every fault, consider cautiously whether you have a certain preventive or a specific remedy in store for each of them.

Women of literature are much more numerous of late than they were a few years ago. They make a class in society, they fill the public eye, and have acquired a degree of consequence and an appropriate character. The esteem of private friends, and the admiration of the public for their talents, are circumstances highly flattering to their vanity; and as such I will allow them to be substantial pleasures. I am also ready to acknowledge that a taste for literature adds much to the happiness of life, and that women may enjoy to a certain degree this happiness as well as men. But with literary women this silent happiness seems at best but a subordinate consideration; it is not by the treasures they possess, but by those which they have an opportunity of displaying, that they estimate their wealth. To obtain public applause, they are betrayed too often into a miserable ostentation of their learning. Coxe tells us, that certain Russian ladies split their pearls, in order to make a greater display of finery.[8]

The pleasure of being admired for wit or erudition, I cannot exactly measure in a female mind; but state it to be as delightful as you can imagine it to be, there are evils attendant upon it, which, in the estimation of a prudent father, may overbalance the good. The intoxicating effect of wit upon the brain has been well remarked, by a poet, who was a friend to the fair sex:[9] and too many ridiculous, and too many disgusting examples confirm the truth of the observation. The deference that is paid to genius, sometimes makes the fair sex forget that genius will be respected only when united with discretion. Those who have acquired fame, fancy that they can afford to sacrifice reputation. I will suppose, however, that their heads shall be strong enough to bear inebriating admiration, and that their conduct shall be essentially irreproachable; yet they will show in their manners and conversation that contempt of inferior minds, and that neglect of common forms and customs, which will provoke the indignation of fools, and which cannot escape the censure of the wise. Even whilst we are secure of their innocence, we dislike that daring spirit in the female sex, which delights to oppose the common opinions of society, and from apparent trifles we draw unfavourable omens, which experience too often confirms. You will ask me why I should suppose that wits are more liable to be spoiled by admiration than beauties, who have usually a larger share of it, and who are not more exempt from vanity? Those who are vain of trifling accomplishments, of rank, of riches, or of beauty, depend upon the world for their immediate gratification. They are sensible of their dependence; they listen with deference to the maxims, and attend with anxiety to the opinions of those, from whom they expect their reward and their daily amusements. In their subjection consists their safety; whilst women, who neither feel dependent for amusement nor for self-approbation upon company and public places, are apt to consider this subjection as humiliating, if not insupportable: perceiving their own superiority, they despise, and even set at defiance, the opinions of their acquaintance of inferior abilities: contempt, where it cannot be openly retorted, produces aversion, not the less to be dreaded because constrained to silence: envy, considered as the involuntary tribute extorted by merit, is flattering to pride: and I know that many women delight to excite envy, even whilst they affect to fear its consequences: but they, who imprudently provoke it, are little aware of the torments they prepare for themselves. − "Cover your face well before you disturb the hornet's nest," was a maxim of the *experienced* Catherine de Medici.[10]

Men of literature, if we may trust to the bitter expressions of anguish in their writings, and in their private letters, feel acutely all the stings of envy. Women, who have more susceptibility of temper, and less strength of mind, and who, from the delicate nature of their reputation, are more exposed to attack, are also less able to endure it. Malignant critics, when they cannot attack an author's peace in his writings, frequently scrutinize his private life; and every personal anecdote is published without regard to truth or propriety. How will the delicacy of the female character endure this treatment? How will her friends bear to see her pursued even in domestic retirement, if she should be wise enough to make that retirement her choice? How will they like to see premature memoirs, and spurious collections of familiar letters, published by needy booksellers, or designing enemies? Yet to all these things men of letters are subject; and such must literary ladies expect, if they attain to any degree of eminence. − Judging, then, from the experience of our sex, I may pronounce envy to be one of the evils which women of uncommon genius have to dread. "Censure," says a celebrated writer, "is a tax which every man must pay to the public, who seeks to be eminent." Women must expect to pay it doubly.[11]

Your daughter, perhaps, shall be above scandal. She shall despise the idle whisper, and the common tattle of her sex; her soul shall be raised above the ignorant and the frivolous; she shall have a relish for higher conversation, and a taste for higher society; but where is she to find, or how is she to obtain this society? You make her incapable of friendship with her own sex. Where is she to look for friends, for companions, for equals? Amongst men? Amongst what class of men? Not amongst men of business, or men of gallantry, but amongst men of literature.[12]

Learned men have usually chosen for their wives, or for their companions, women who were rather below than above the standard of mediocrity: this seems to me natural and reasonable. Such men, probably, feel their own incapacity for the daily business of life, their ignorance of the world, their slovenly habits, and neglect of domestic affairs. They do not want wives who have precisely their own defects; they rather desire to find such as shall, by the opposite habits and virtues, supply their deficiencies. I do not see why two books should marry, any more than two estates. Some few exceptions might be quoted against Stewart's observations. I have just seen, under the article "A Literary Wife", in D'Israeli's *Curiosities of Literature*,[13] an account of Francis Phidelphus, a great scholar in the fifteenth century, who was so desirous of acquiring the Greek language in perfection, that he travelled to Constantinople in search of a *Grecian wife*: the lady proved a scold. "But to do justice to the name of Theodora," as this author adds, "she has been honourably mentioned in the French Academy of Sciences." I hope this proved an adequate compensation to her husband for his domestic broils.

Happy Mad. Dacier![14] you found a husband suited to your taste! You and Mons. Dacier, if D'Alembert[15] tells the story rightly, once cooked a dish in concert, by a receipt which you found in Apicius and you both sat down and ate of your learned ragout till you were both like to die.[16]

Were I sure, my dear friend, that every literary lady would be equally fortunate in finding in a husband a man who would sympathize in her tastes, I should diminish my formidable catalogue of evils. But, alas! M. Dacier is no more; "and we shall never live to see his fellow."[17] Literary ladies will, I am afraid, be losers in love, as well as in friendship, by the superiority. – Cupid is a timid, playful child, and is frightened at the helmet of Minerva. It has been observed, that gentlemen are not apt to admire a prodigious quantity of learning and masculine acquirements in the fair sex; – we usually consider a certain degree of weakness, both of mind and body, as friendly to female grace. I am not absolutely of this opinion; yet I do not see the advantage of supernatural force, either of body or mind, to female excellence. Hercules-Spinster found his strength rather an incumbrance than an advantage.[18]

Superiority of mind must be united with great temper and generosity, to be tolerated by those who are forced to submit to its influence. I have seen witty and learned ladies, who did not seem to think it at all incumbent upon them to sacrifice any thing to the sense of propriety. On the contrary, they seemed to take both pride and pleasure in showing the utmost stretch of their strength, regardless of the consequences, panting only for victory. Upon such occasions, when the adversary has been a husband or a father, I must acknowledge that I have felt sensations which few ladies can easily believe they excite. Airs and graces I can bear as well as another; but airs without graces no man thinks himself bound to bear, and learned airs least of all. Ladies of high rank in the court of Parnassus[19] are apt, sometimes, to claim precedency out of their own dominions, which creates much confusion, and generally ends in their being affronted. That knowledge of the world which keeps people in their proper places they will never learn from the Muses.

Molière has pointed out, with all the force of comic ridicule, in the *Femmes Savantes*, that a lady, who aspires to the sublime delights of philosophy and poetry, must forego the simple pleasures, and will despise the duties of domestic life.[20] I should not expect that my house affairs would be with haste despatched by a Desdemona, weeping over some unvarnished tale, or petrified with some history of horrors, at the very time when she should be ordering dinner, or paying the butcher's bill.[21] – I should have the less hope of rousing her attention to my culinary concerns and domestic grievances, because I should probably incur her contempt for hinting at these sublunary matters, and her indignation for supposing that she ought to be employed in such degrading occupations. I have heard, that if these sublime geniuses are awakened from their reveries by the *appulse* of external circumstances, they start, and exhibit all the perturbation and amazement of *cataleptic* patients.[22]

Sir Charles Harrington, in the days of Queen Elizabeth, addressed a copy of verses to his wife, "On Women's Vertues": – these he divides into "the private, *civill*, and heroyke"; the private belong to the country housewife, whom it concerneth chiefly –

> The fruit, malt, hops, to tend, to dry, to utter,
>> To beat, strip, spin the wool, the hemp, the flax,
>> Breed poultry, gather honey, try the wax,
> And more than all, to have good cheese and butter.
> Then next a step, but yet a large step higher,
>> Came civill vertue fitter for the citty,
>> With modest looks, good clothes, and answers witty.
> These baser things not done, but guided by her.

As for heroyke vertue, and heroyke dames, honest Sir Charles would have nothing to do with them.[23]

Allowing, however, that you could combine all these virtues – that you could form a perfect whole, a female wonder from every creature's best – dangers still threaten you. How will you preserve your daughter from that desire of universal admiration, which will ruin all your work? How will you, along with all the pride of knowledge, give her that "retiring modesty", which is supposed to have more charms for our sex than the fullest display of wit and beauty?

The *fair Pauca of Thoulouse* was so called because she was so fair that no one could live either with or without beholding her – whenever she came forth from her own mansion, which, history observes, she did very seldom, such impetuous crowds rushed to obtain a sight of her, that limbs were broken and lives were lost wherever she appeared. She ventured abroad less frequently – the evil increased – till at length the magistrates of the city issued an edict commanding the fair Pauca, under the pain of perpetual imprisonment, to appear in broad daylight for one hour, every week, in the public market-place.

Modern ladies, by frequenting public places so regularly, declare their approbation of the wholesome regulations of these prudent magistrates. Very different was the crafty policy of the prophet Mahomet, who forbad his worshippers even to paint his picture. The Turks have pictures of the hand, the foot, the features of Mahomet, but no representation of the whole face or person is allowed. The portraits of our beauties, in our exhibition-room, show a proper contempt of this insidious policy; and those learned and ingenious ladies who publish their private letters, select maxims, secret anecdotes, and family memoirs, are entitled to our thanks, for thus presenting us with full-lengths of their minds.

Can you expect, my dear sir, that your daughter, with all the genius and learning which you intend to give her, should refrain from these imprudent exhibitions? Will she "yield her charms of mind with sweet delay"? Will she, in every moment of her life, recollect that the fatal desire for universal applause always defeats its own purpose, especially if the purpose be to win our love as well as our admiration? It is in vain to tell me, that more enlarged ideas in our sex would alter our tastes, and alter even the associations which now influence our passions. The captive who has numbered the links of his chains, and has even discovered how those chains are constructed, is not therefore nearer to the recovery of his liberty.

Besides, it must take a length of time to alter associations and opinions, which, if not *just*, are at least *common* in our sex. You cannot expect even that conviction should operate immediately upon the public taste. You will, in a few years, have educated your daughter; and if the world be not educated exactly at the right time to judge of her perfections, to admire and love them, you will have wasted your labour, and you will have sacrificed your daughter's happiness: that happiness, analyze it as a man of the world or as a philosopher, must depend on friendship, love, the exercise of her virtues, the just performance of all the duties of life, and the self-approbation arising from the consciousness of good conduct.

I am, my dear friend,
Yours sincerely.

ANSWER TO THE PRECEDING LETTER

I have as little taste for Mad. Dacier's learned ragout as you can have, my dear sir; and I pity the great scholar, who travelled to Constantinople for the termagant Theodora, believing, as you do, that the honourable mention made of her by the French Academy of Sciences, could be no adequate compensation to her husband for domestic disquiet: but the lady's learning was not essential to his misfortune; he might have met with a scolding dame, though he had not married a Grecian. A profusion of vulgar aphorisms in the dialects of all the counties in England, proverbs in Welsh, Scotish, French, Spanish, Italian, and Hebrew, might be adduced to prove that scolds are to be found amongst all classes of women. I am, however, willing to allow, that the more learning, and wit, and eloquence a lady possesses, the more troublesome and the more dangerous she may become as a wife or daughter, unless she is also possessed of good sense and good temper. Of your honest Sir Charles Harrington's two pattern wives, I think I should prefer the country housewife, with whom I could be sure of having good cheese and butter, to the *citty dame* with her good clothes and answers witty. − I should be afraid that these answers witty might be turned against me, and might prove the torment of my life. − You, who have attended to female disputants, must have remarked, that, learned or unlearned, they seldom know how to reason; they assert and declaim, employ wit, and eloquence, and sophistry, to confute, persuade, or abash their adversaries; but distinct reasoning they neither use nor comprehend. − Till women learn to reason, it is in vain that they acquire learning.

You are satisfied, I am sure, with this acknowledgment. I will go farther, and at once give up to you all the learned ladies that exist, or that ever have existed: but when I use the term literary ladies, I mean women who have cultivated their understandings not for the purposes of parade, but with the desire to make themselves useful and agreeable. I estimate the value of a woman's abilities and acquirements, by the degree in which they contribute to her happiness.

You think yourself happy because you are wise, said a philosopher to a pedant. – I think myself wise because I am happy.

You tell me, that even supposing I could educate my daughter so as to raise her above the common faults and follies of her sex; even supposing I could give her an enlarged understanding, and literature free from pedantry, she would be in danger of becoming unhappy, because she would not, amongst her own sex, find friends suited to her taste, nor amongst ours, admirers adequate to her expectations: you represent her as in the situation of the poor flying-fish, exposed to dangerous enemies in her own element, yet certain, if she tries to soar above them, of being pounced upon by the hawk-eyed critics of the higher regions.

You allow, however, that women of literature are much more numerous of late than they were a few years ago; that they make a class in society, and have acquired a considerable degree of consequence, and an appropriate character; how can you then fear that a woman of cultivated understanding should be driven from the society of her own sex in search of dangerous companions amongst ours? In the female world she will be neither without an equal nor without a judge; she will not have much to fear from envy, because its malignant eye will not fix upon one object exclusively, when there are numbers to distract its attention, and share the stroke. The fragile nature of female friendships, the petty jealousies which break out at the ball or in the drawing-room, have been from time immemorial the jest of mankind. Trifles, light as air, will necessarily excite not only the jealousy, but the envy of those who think only of trifles. Give them more employment for their thoughts, give them a nobler spirit of emulation, and we shall hear no more of these paltry feuds; give them more useful and more interesting subjects of conversation, and they become not only more agreeable, but safer companions for each other.

Unmarried women, who have stored their minds with knowledge, who have various tastes and literary occupations, who can amuse and be amused in the conversation of well-informed people, are in no danger of becoming burthensome to their friends or to society: though they may not be seen haunting every place of amusement or of public resort, they are not isolated or forlorn; by a variety of associations they are connected with the world, and their sympathy is expanded and supported by the cultivation of their understandings; nor can it sink, settle, and concentrate upon cats, parrots, and monkeys.[24] How far the human heart may be contracted by ignorance it is difficult to determine; but I am little inclined to envy the *simple* pleasures of those whose understandings are totally uncultivated. – Sir William Hamilton, in his account of the last eruption of Mount Vesuvius, gives us a curious picture of the excessive ignorance and stupidity of some nuns in a convent at Torre del Greco: – one of these nuns was found warming herself at the red-hot lava, which had rolled up to the window of her cell. It was with the greatest difficulty that these scarcely rational beings could be made to comprehend the nature of their danger; and when at last they were prevailed upon to quit the convent, and were advised to carry with them whatever they thought most valuable, they loaded themselves with sweetmeats.[25] – Those who wish for ignorant wives, may find them in other parts of the world, as well as in Italy.

I do not pretend, that even by cultivating my daughter's understanding I can secure for her a husband suited to her taste; it will therefore be prudent to make her felicity in some degree independent of matrimony. Many parents have sufficient kindness and foresight to provide, in point of fortune, for their daughters; but few consider that if a single life should be their choice or their doom, something more is necessary to secure respect and happiness for them in the decline of life. The silent *unreproved* pleasures of literature are the sure resource of those who have cultivated minds; those who have not, must wear out their disconsolate unoccupied old age as chance directs.

When you say that men of superior understanding dislike the appearance of extraordinary strength of mind in the fair sex, you probably mean that the display of that strength is disgusting, and you associate with the idea of strength of mind, masculine, arrogant, or pedantic manners: but there is no necessary connexion between these things; and it seems probable that the faults usually ascribed to learned ladies, like those peculiar to learned men, may have arisen in a great measure from circumstances which the progress of civilization in society has much altered.

In the times of ignorance, men of deep science were considered by the vulgar as a class of necromancers,[26] and they were looked upon alternately with terror and admiration; and learned men imposed upon the vulgar by assuming strange airs of mystery and self-importance, wore long beards and solemn looks; they spoke and wrote in a phraseology peculiar to themselves, and affected to consider the rest of mankind as beneath their notice: but since knowledge has been generally diffused, all this affectation has been laid aside; and though we now and then hear of men of genius who indulge themselves in peculiarities, yet upon the whole the manners of literary men are not strikingly nor wilfully different from those of the rest of the world. The peculiarities of literary women will also disappear as their numbers increase. You are disgusted by their ostentation of learning. Have patience with them, my dear sir; their taste will become more simple when they have been taught by experience that this parade is offensive: even the bitter expression of your disgust may be advantageous to those whose manners are yet to be formed; they will at least learn from it what to avoid; and your letter may perhaps hereafter be of service in my daughter's education. – It is scarcely to be supposed, that a girl of good understanding would deliberately imitate the faults and follies which she hears ridiculed during her childhood, by those whom she esteems.

As to your dread of prodigies, that will subside: – prodigies are heard of most frequently during the ages of ignorance.[27] A woman may now possess a considerable stock of information without being gazed upon as a miracle of learning; and there is not much danger of her being vain of accomplishments which cease to be astonishing. Nor will her peace be disturbed by the idle remarks of the ignorant vulgar. – A literary lady is no longer a sight; the spectacle is now too common to attract curiosity; the species of animal is too well known even to admit of much exaggeration in the description of its appearance. A lady riding on horseback upon a side-saddle is not thought a wonderful thing by the common people in England; but when an English lady rode upon a side-saddle in an Italian city, where the sight was unusual, she was universally gazed at by the populace; to some she appeared an object of astonishment, to others of compassion: – "Ah! poverina," they exclaimed, "n'ha che una gamba!"[28]

The same objects excite different emotions in different situations; and to judge what will astonish or delight any given set of people some years hence, we must consider not merely what is the fashion of to-day, but whither the current of opinion runs, and what is likely to be the fashion of hereafter. – You must have observed that public opinion is at present more favourable to the cultivation of the understanding of the female sex than it was some years ago; more attention is paid to the education of women, more knowledge and literature are expected from them in society. From the literary lady of the present day something more is expected than that she should know how to spell and to write better than Swift's celebrated Stella, whom he reproves for writing *villian* and *daenger*: – perhaps this very Stella was an object of envy in her own day to those who were her inferiors in literature.[29] No man wishes his wife to be obviously less cultivated than those of her own rank; and something more is now required, even from ordinary talents, than what distinguished the accomplished lady of the seventeenth century. What the standard of excellence may be in the next age we cannot ascertain, but we may guess that the taste for literature will continue to be progressive; therefore, even if you assume that the education of the female sex should be guided by the taste and reigning opinions of ours, and that it should be the object of their lives to win and keep our hearts, you must admit the expediency of attending to that fashionable demand for literature and the fine arts, which has arisen in society.

No woman can foresee what may be the taste of the man with whom she may be united; much of her happiness, however, will depend upon her being able to conform her taste to his: for this reason I should therefore, in female education, cultivate the general powers of the mind, rather than any particular faculty. I do not desire to make my daughter merely a musician, a painter, or a poet; I do not desire to make her merely a botanist, a mathematician, or a chemist; but I wish to give her early the habit of industry and attention, the love of knowledge, and the power of reasoning: these will enable her to attend to excellence in any pursuit to which she may direct her talents. You will observe, that many things which formerly were thought above the comprehension of women, or unfit for their sex, are now acknowledged to be perfectly within the compass of their abilities, and suited to their situation. — Formerly the fair sex was kept in Turkish ignorance;[30] every means of acquiring knowledge was discountenanced by fashion, and impracticable even to those who despised fashion; — our books of science were full of unintelligible jargon, and mystery veiled pompous ignorance from public contempt: but now writers must offer their discoveries to the public in distinct terms, which every body may understand; technical language no longer supplies the place of knowledge, and the art of teaching has been carried to such perfection, that a degree of knowledge may now with ease be acquired in the course of a few years, which formerly it was the business of a life to attain. All this is much in favour of female literature. Ladies have become ambitious to superintend the education of their children, and hence they have been induced to instruct themselves, that they may be able to direct and inform their pupils. The mother, who now aspires to be the esteemed and beloved instructress of her children, must have a considerable portion of knowledge. Science has of late "*been enlisted under the banners of imagination*", by the irresistible charms of genius; by the same power, her votaries will be led "*from the looser analogies which dress out the imagery of poetry to the stricter ones which form the ratiocination of philosophy.*"[31] — Botany has become fashionable; in time it may become useful, if it be not so already. Chemistry will follow botany. Chemistry is a science well suited to the talents and situation of women; it is not a science of parade; it affords occupation and infinite variety; it demands no bodily strength; it can be pursued in retirement; it applies immediately to useful and domestic purposes: and whilst the ingenuity of the most inventive mind may in this science be exercised, there is no danger of inflaming the imagination, because the mind is intent upon realities, the knowledge that is acquired is exact, and the pleasure of the pursuit is a sufficient reward for the labour.

A clear and ready knowledge of arithmetic is surely no useless acquirement for those who are to regulate the expenses of a family. Economy is not the mean "penny wise and pound foolish" policy which some suppose it to be;[32] it is the art of calculation joined to the habit of order, and the power of proportioning our wishes to the means of gratifying them. The little pilfering temper of a wife[33] is despicable and odious to every man of sense; but there is a judicious, graceful species of economy, which has no connexion with an avaricious temper, and which, as it depends upon the understanding, can be expected only from cultivated minds. Women who have been well educated, far from despising domestic duties, will hold them in high respect; because they will see that the whole happiness of life is made up of the happiness of each particular day and hour, and that much of the enjoyment of these must depend upon the punctual practice of those virtues which are more valuable than splendid.

It is not, I hope, your opinion, that ignorance is the best security for female virtue. If this connexion between virtue and ignorance could once be clearly proved, we ought to drown our books deeper than ever plummet sounded: — I say *we* — for the danger extends equally to both sexes, unless you assert that the

duties of men rest upon a more certain foundation than the
duties of the other sex: if our virtues can be demonstrated to be
advantageous, why should theirs suffer for being exposed to the
light of reason? – All social virtue conduces to our own
happiness or that of our fellow-creatures; can it weaken the
sense of duty to illustrate this truth? – Having once pointed out
to the understanding of a sensible woman the necessary
connexion between her virtues and her happiness, must not
those virtues, and the means of preserving them, become in her
eyes objects of the most interesting importance? But you fear,
that even if their conduct continued to be irreproachable, the
manners of women might be rendered less delicate by the
increase of their knowledge; you dislike in the female sex that
daring spirit which despises the common forms of society, and
which breaks through the reserve and delicacy of female
manners: – so do I: – and the best method to make my pupil
respect these things is to show her how they are indispensably
connected with the largest interests of society: surely this
perception of the utility of forms apparently trifling, must be a
strong security to the prudential reserve of the sex, and far
superior to the automatic habits of those who submit to the
conventions of the world without consideration or conviction.
Habit, confirmed by reason, assumes the rank of virtue. The
motives that restrain from vice must be increased by the clear
conviction, that vice and wretchedness are inseparably united.

Do not, however, imagine, my dear sir, that I shall attempt to
lay moral demonstration before *a child*, who could not possibly
comprehend my meaning; do not imagine that because I intend
to cultivate my daughter's understanding, I shall neglect to give
her those early habits of reserve and modesty which constitute
the female character. – Believing, as I do, that woman, as well as
man, may be called a bundle of habits, I shall be peculiarly
careful, during my child's early education, to give her as many
good habits as possible; by degrees as her understanding, that is
to say as her knowledge and power of reasoning shall increase, I
can explain the advantages of these habits, and confirm their
power by the voice of reason. I lose no time, I expose myself to no

danger, by this system. On the contrary, those who depend entirely upon the force of custom and prejudice expose themselves to infinite danger. If once their pupils begin to reflect upon their own hoodwinked education, they will probably suspect that they have been deceived in all that they have been taught, and they will burst their bonds with indignation. – Credulity is always rash in the moment she detects the impositions that have been practised upon her easy temper. In this inquiring age, few have any chance of passing through life without being excited to examine the motives and principles from which they act: is it not therefore prudent to cultivate the reasoning faculty, by which alone this examination can be made with safety? A false argument, a repartee, the charms of wit or eloquence, the voice of fashion, of folly, of numbers, might, if she had no substantial reasons to support her cause, put virtue not only out of countenance, but out of humour.

You speak of moral instinct. As far as I understand the term, it implies certain habits early acquired from education; to these I would add the power of reasoning, and then, and not till then, I should think myself safe: – for I have observed that the pupils of habit are utterly confounded when they are placed in circumstances different from those to which they have been accustomed. – It has been remarked by travellers and naturalists, that animals, notwithstanding their boasted instinctive knowledge, sometimes make strange and fatal mistakes in their conduct, when they are placed in new situations:– destitute of the reasoning faculty, and deceived by resemblances, they mistake poison for food. Thus the bull-frog will swallow burning charcoal, mistaking it for fire-flies; and the European hogs and poultry which travelled to Surinam poisoned themselves by eating plants that were unknown to them.[34]

You seem, my dear sir, to be afraid that truth should not keep so firm a hold upon the mind as prejudice; and you produce an allusion to justify your fears. You tell us that civil society is like a building, and you warn me not to tear down the ivy which clings to the walls, and braces the loose stones together. – I believe that ivy, in some situations, tends to pull down the walls to which it clings. – You think it is not worth while to cultivate the understandings of women, because you say that you have no security that the conviction of their reason will have any permanent good effect upon their conduct; and to persuade me of this, you bid me observe that men who are superior to women in strength of mind and judgment, are frequently misled by their passions. By this mode of argument, you may conclude that reason is totally useless to the whole human race; but you cannot, with any show of justice, infer that it ought to be monopolized by one-half of mankind. But why should you quarrel with reason, because passion sometimes conquers her? – You should endeavour to strengthen the connexion between theory and practice, if it be not sufficiently strong already; but you can gain nothing by destroying theory. – Happiness is your aim; but your unpractised or unsteady hand does not obey your will: you do not at the first trial hit the mark precisely. – Would you, because you are awkward, insist upon being blind?

The strength of mind which enables people to govern themselves by their reason, is not always connected with abilities even in their most cultivated state: I deplore the instances which I have seen of this truth, but I do not despair; on the contrary, I am excited to inquire into the causes of this phenomenon; nor, because I see some evil, would I sacrifice the good upon a bare motive of suspicion. It is a contradiction to say, that giving the power to discern what is good is giving a disposition to prefer what is bad. I acknowledge with regret, that women who have been but half instructed, who have seen only superficially the relations of moral and political ideas, and who have obtained but an imperfect knowledge of the human heart, have conducted themselves so as to disgrace their talents and their sex; these are conspicuous and melancholy examples, which are cited oftener with malice than with pity. But I appeal to examples amongst our contemporaries, to which every man of literature will immediately advert, to prove, that where the female understanding has been properly cultivated, women have not only obtained admiration by their useful abilities, but respect by their exemplary conduct.[35]

I apprehend that many of the errors into which women of literature have fallen, may have arisen from an improper choice of books. Those who read chiefly works of imagination, receive from them false ideas of life and of the human heart. Many of these productions I should keep as I would deadly poison from my child; I should rather endeavour to turn her attention to science than to romance, and to give her early that taste for truth and utility, which, when once implanted, can scarcely be eradicated. There is a wide difference between innocence and ignorance: ignorant women may have minds the most debased and perverted, whilst the most cultivated understanding may be united with the most perfect innocence and simplicity.

Even if literature were of no other use to the fair sex than to supply them with employment, I should think the time dedicated to the cultivation of their minds well bestowed: they are surely better occupied when they are reading or writing than when coqueting or gaming, losing their fortunes or their characters. You despise the writings of women: – you think that they might have made a better use of the pen, than to write plays, and poetry, and romances. Considering that the pen was to women a new instrument, I think they have made at least as good a use of it as learned men did of the needle some centuries ago, when they set themselves to determine how many spirits could stand upon its point, and were ready to tear one another to pieces in the discussion of this sublime question.[36] Let the sexes mutually forgive each other their follies; or, what is much better, let them combine their talents for their general advantage. — You say, that the experiments we have made do not encourage us to proceed – that the increased care and pains which have been of late years bestowed upon female education have produced no adequate returns; but you in the same breath allow that amongst your contemporaries, whom you prudently forbear to mention, there are some instances of great talents applied to useful purposes. Did you expect that the fruits of good cultivation should appear before the seed was sown? You triumphantly enumerate the disadvantages to which women, from the laws and customs of society, are liable: – they cannot converse freely with men of wit, science, and learning, nor even with the artist, or artificers; they are excluded from academies, public libraries, &c. Even our politeness prevents us, you say, from ever speaking plain truth and sense to the fair sex: – every assistance that foreign or domestic ingenuity can invent to encourage literary studies, is, as you boast, almost exclusively ours: and after pointing out all these causes for the inferiority of women in knowledge, you ask for a list of the inventions and discoveries of those who, by your own statement of the question, have not been allowed opportunities for observation. With the insulting injustice of an Egyptian task-master, you demand the work, and deny the necessary materials.

I admit, that with respect to the opportunities of acquiring knowledge, institutions and manners are, as you have stated, much in favour of our sex; but your argument concerning *time* appears to me to be unfounded. – Women who do not love dissipation must have more time for the cultivation of their understandings than men can have, if you compute the whole of life: – whilst the knowledge of the learned languages continues to form an indispensable part of a gentleman's education, many years of childhood and youth must be devoted to their attainment. – During these studies, the general cultivation of the understanding is in some degree retarded. All the intellectual powers are cramped, except the memory, which is sufficiently exercised, but which is overloaded with words, and with words that are not always understood. – The genius of living and of dead languages differs so much, that the pains which are taken to write elegant Latin frequently spoil the English style. – Girls usually write much better than boys; they think and express their thoughts clearly at an age when young men can scarcely write an easy letter upon any common occasion. Women do not read the good authors of antiquity as school-books, but they can have excellent translations of most of them when they are capable of tasting the beauties of composition. – I know that it is supposed we cannot judge of the classics by translations, and I am sensible that much of the merit of the originals may be lost; but I think the difference in pleasure is more than overbalanced to women by the *time* that is saved, and by the labour and misapplication of abilities which are spared. If they do not acquire a classical taste, neither do they imbibe classic prejudices; nor are they early disgusted with literature by pedagogues, lexicons, grammars, and all the melancholy apparatus of learning. – Women begin to taste the pleasures of reading, and the best authors in the English language are their amusement, just at the age when young men, disgusted by their studies, begin to be ashamed of alluding to literature amongst their companions. Travelling, lounging, field sports, gaming, and what is called pleasure in various shapes, usually fill the interval between quitting the university and settling for life. – When this period is past, business, the necessity of pursuing a profession, the ambition to shine in parliament, or to rise in public life, occupy a large portion of their lives. – In many professions the understanding is but partially cultivated; and general literature must be neglected by those who are occupied in earning bread or amassing riches for their family: – men of genius are often heard to complain, that in the pursuit of a profession, they are obliged to contract their inquiries and concentrate their powers; statesmen lament that they must often pursue the *expedient* even when they discern that it is not *the right*; and men of letters, who earn their bread by their writings, inveigh bitterly against the tyranny of booksellers, who degrade them to the state of "literary artisans". — "Literary artisans," is the comprehensive term under which a celebrated philosopher classes all those who cultivate only particular talents or powers of the mind, and who suffer their other faculties to lose all strength and vigour for want of exercise.[37] The other sex have no such constraint upon their understandings; neither the necessity of earning their bread, nor the ambition to shine in public affairs, hurry or prejudice their minds: in domestic life they have leisure to be wise.

Far from being ashamed that so little has been done by female abilities in science and useful literature, I am surprised that so much has been effected. On natural history, on criticism, on moral philosophy, on education, they have written with elegance, eloquence, precision, and ingenuity. Your complaint that women do not turn their attention to useful literature is surely ill-timed. If they merely increased the number of books in circulation, you might declaim against them with success; but when they add to the general fund of useful and entertaining knowledge, you cannot with any show of justice prohibit their labours: there can be no danger that the market should ever be overstocked with produce of intrinsic worth.

The despotic monarchs of Spain forbid the exploring of any new gold or silver mines without the express permission of government, and they have ordered several rich ones to be shut up as not equal to the cost of working. There is some *appearance* of reason for this exertion of power: it may prevent the world from being encumbered by nominal wealth. – But the Dutch merchants, who burn whole cargoes of spice lest they should lower the price of the commodity in which they deal, show a mean spirit of monopoly which can plead no plausible excuse.[38] – I hope you feel nothing like a disposition to Spanish despotism or Dutch jealousy, when you would exclude female talents from the literary market.

You observe, that since censure is a tax which every man must pay who aspires to eminence, women must expect to pay it doubly. Why the tax should not be equally assessed, I am at a loss to conjecture: but in fact it does not fall very heavy upon those who have any portion of philosophy: they may, with *the poet of reason*, exclaim –

> Though doubly tax'd, how little have I lost!

Your dread of the envy attendant upon literary excellence might with equal justice be extended to every species of merit, and might be urged against all that is good in art or nature. – Scandal is said to attack always the fairest characters, as the birds always peck most at the ripest fruit; but would you for this reason have no fruit ripen, or no characters aspire to excellence?

But if it be your opinion that women are naturally inferior to us in capacity, why do you feel so much apprehension of their becoming eminent, or of their obtaining power, in consequence of the cultivation of their understandings? – These expressions of scorn and jealousy neutralize each other. If your contempt were unmixed and genuine, it would be cool and tranquil, inclining rather to pity than to anger.

You say that in all animals the female is the inferior; and you have never seen any reason to believe that the human species affords an exception to this observation. – Superiority amongst brutes depends upon force; superiority amongst the human species depends upon reason: that men are naturally stronger than women is evident; but strength of mind has no necessary connexion with strength of body; and intellectual ability has ever conquered mere physical force, from the times of Ajax and Ulysses to the present day.[39] In civilized nations, that species of superiority which belongs to force is much reduced in value amongst the higher classes of society. – The baron who struck his sword into an oak, and defied any one to pull out the weapon, would not in these days fill the hearts of his antagonists with terror; nor would the twisting of a horseshoe be deemed a feat worthy to decide a nation in their choice of a king.[40] – The days of chivalry are no more: the knight no longer sallies forth in ponderous armour, mounted upon "a steed as invulnerable as himself."[41] – The damsel no longer depends upon the prowess of his mighty arm to maintain the glory of her charms, or the purity of her fame; grim barons, and castles guarded by monsters and all-devouring dragons, are no more; and from being the champions and masters of the fair sex, we are now become their friends and companions. We have not surely been losers by this change; the fading glories of romance have vanished, but the real permanent pleasures of domestic life remain in their stead; and what the fair have lost of adulation they have gained in friendship.

Do not, my dear sir, call me a champion for the rights of woman;[42] I am too much their friend to be their partisan, and I am more anxious for their happiness than intent upon a metaphysical discussion of their rights: their happiness is so nearly connected with ours, that it seems to me absurd to manage any argument so as to set the two sexes at variance by vain contention for superiority. It ought not to be our object to make an invidious division of privileges, or an ostentatious declaration of rights, but to determine what is most for our general advantage.

You fear that the minds of women should be enlarged and cultivated, lest their power in society and their liberty should consequently increase. Observe that the word *liberty*, applied to the female sex, conveys alarming ideas to our minds, because we do not stay to define the term; we have a confused notion that it implies want of reserve, want of delicacy; boldness of manners, or of conduct; in short, liberty to do wrong. – Surely this is a species of liberty which knowledge can never make desirable. Those who understand the real interests of society, who clearly see the connexion between virtue and happiness, must know that *the liberty to do wrong* is synonymous with *the liberty to make themselves miserable*. This is a privilege of which none would choose to avail themselves. When reason defines the term, there is no danger of its being misunderstood; but imagination and false associations often make this word liberty, in its perverted sense, sound delightful to those who have been kept in ignorance and slavery. Girls who have been disciplined under the strict high hand of authority, are apt to fancy that to escape from habitual restraint, to exercise their own will, no matter how, is to be free and to be happy. – Hence innumerable errors in their conduct; hence their mistaken notions of liberty, and that inordinate ambition to acquire power, which ignorant, ill-educated women show in every petty struggle, where they are permitted to act in private life. You believe this temper to be inherent in the sex; and a man, who has just published a book upon the Spanish bull-fights, declares his belief, that the passion for bull-fighting is innate in the breast of every Spaniard. – Do not, my friend, assign two causes for an effect where one is obviously adequate. The disposition to love command need not be attributed to any innate cause in the minds of females, whilst it may be fairly ascribed to their erroneous education.

I shall early cultivate my daughter's judgment, to prevent her from being wilful or positive; I shall leave her to choose for herself in all those trifles upon which the happiness of childhood depends; and I shall gradually teach her to reflect upon the consequences of her actions, to compare and judge of her feelings, and to compute the morn and evening to her day. — I shall thus, I hope, induce her to reason upon all subjects, even upon matters of taste, where many women think it sufficient to say, I admire; or, I detest: — Oh, charming! or, Oh, horrible! — People who have reasons for their preferences and aversions, are never so provokingly zealous in the support of their own tastes, as those usually are who have no arguments to convince themselves or others that they are in the right.

But you are apprehensive that the desire to govern, which women show in domestic life, should obtain a larger field to display itself in public affairs. — It seems to me impossible that they can ever acquire the species of direct power which you dread: their influence must be private; it is therefore of the utmost consequence that it should be judicious. — It was not Themistocles, but his wife and child, who governed the Athenians;[43] it was therefore of some consequence that the boy who governed the mother, who governed her husband, should not be a spoiled child; and consequently that the mother who educated this child should be a reasonable woman. Thus are human affairs chained together; and female influence is a necessary and important link, which you cannot break without destroying the whole.

If it be your object, my dear sir, to monopolize power for our sex, you cannot possibly secure it better from the wishes of the other, than by enlightening their minds and enlarging their views: they will then be convinced, not by the voice of the moralist, who puts us to sleep whilst he persuades us of the vanity of all sublunary enjoyments, but by their own awakened observation: they will be convinced that power is generally an evil to its possessor; that to those who really wish for the good of their fellow-creatures, it is at best but a painful trust. — The mad philosopher in Rasselas, who imagined that he regulated the weather and distributed the seasons, could never enjoy a moment's repose, lest he should not make "to the different nations of the earth an impartial dividend of rain and sunshine."[44] – Those who are entrusted with the government of nations must, if they have an acute sense of justice, experience something like the anxiety felt by this unfortunate monarch of the clouds.

Lord Kenyon has lately decided that a woman may *be an overseer of a parish*;[45] but you are not, I suppose, apprehensive that many ladies of cultivated understanding should become ambitious of this honour. – One step farther in reasoning, and a woman would desire as little to be a queen or an empress, as to be the overseer of a parish. – You may perhaps reply, that men, even those of the greatest understanding, have been ambitious, and fond even to excess of power. That ambition is the glorious fault of heroes, I allow; but heroes are not always men of the most enlarged understandings – they are possessed by the spirit of military adventure – an infectious spirit, which men catch from one another in the course of their education: – to this contagion the fair sex are not exposed.

At all events, if you suppose that women are likely to acquire influence in the state, it is prudent to enlighten their understandings, that they may not make an absurd or pernicious use of their power. You appeal to history, to prove that great calamities have ensued whenever the female sex has obtained power; yet you acknowledge that we cannot with certainty determine whether these evils have been the effects of our trusting them with liberty, or of our neglecting previously to instruct them in the use of it: – upon the decision of this question rests your whole argument. In a most awful tone of declamation, you bid me follow the history of female nature, from the court of Augustus to that of Louis XIV, and tell you whether I can hesitate to acknowledge, that the liberty and influence of women have always been the greatest during the decline of empires. – But you have not proved to me that women had more knowledge, that they were better educated, at the court of Augustus, or during the reign of Louis XIV, than at any other place, or during any other period of the world; therefore your argument gains nothing by the admission of your assertions; and unless I could trace the history of female education, it is vain for me to follow what you call the history of female nature.

It is, however, remarkable, that the means by which the sex have hitherto obtained that species of power which they have abused, have arisen chiefly from their personal, and not from their mental qualifications; from their skill in the arts of persuasion, and from their accomplishments; not from their superior powers of reasoning, or from the cultivation of their understanding. The most refined species of coquetry can undoubtedly be practised in the highest perfection by women, who to personal graces unite all the fascination of wit and eloquence. There is infinite danger in permitting such women to obtain power without having acquired habits of reasoning. Rousseau admires these sirens; but the system of Rousseau, pursued to its fullest extent, would overturn the world, would make every woman a Cleopatra, and every man an Antony; it would destroy all domestic virtue, all domestic happiness, all the pleasures of truth and love.[46] — In the midst of that delirium of passion to which Antony gave the name of love, what must have been the state of his degraded, wretched soul, when he could suspect his mistress of designs upon his life? – To cure him of these suspicions, she at a banquet poisoned the flowers of his garland, waited till she saw him inflamed with wine, then persuaded him to break the tops of his flowers into his goblet, and just stopped him when the cup was at his lips, exclaiming – "Those flowers are poisoned: you see that I do not want the means of destroying you, if you were become tiresome to me, or if I could live without you." — And this is the happy pair who instituted the orders of *The inimitable lovers*! – and *The companions in death*![47]

These are the circumstances which should early be pointed out, to both sexes, with all the energy of truth: let them learn that the most exquisite arts of the most consummate coquette, could not obtain the confidence of him, who sacrificed to her charms, the empire of the world. It is from the experience of the past that we must form our judgment of the future. How unjustly you accuse me of desiring to destroy the memory of past experiments, the wisdom collected by the labour of ages! *You* would prohibit this treasure of knowledge to one-half of the human species; and *I* on the contrary would lay it open to all my fellow-creatures. – I speak as if it were actually in our option to retard or to accelerate the intellectual progress of the sex; but in fact it is absolutely out of our power to drive the fair sex back to their former state of darkness: the art of printing has totally changed their situation; their eyes are opened, – the classic page is unrolled, they *will* read: – all we can do is to induce them to read with judgment – to enlarge their minds so that they may take a full view of their interests and of ours. I have no fear that the truth upon any subject should injure my daughter's mind; it is falsehood that I dread. I dread that she should acquire preposterous notions of love, of happiness, from the furtive perusal of vulgar novels, or from the clandestine conversation of ignorant waiting-maids: – I dread that she should acquire, even from the enchanting eloquence of Rousseau, the fatal idea, that cunning and address are the natural resources of her sex; that coquetry is necessary to attract, and dissimulation to preserve the heart of man.[48] — I would not, however, proscribe an author, because I believe some of his opinions to be false; I would have my daughter read and compare various books, and correct her judgment of books by listening to the conversation of persons of sense and experience. Women may learn much of what is essential to their happiness, from the unprejudiced testimony of a father or a brother; they may learn to distinguish the pictures of real life from paintings of imaginary manners and passions which never had, which never can have, any existence. – They may learn that it is not the reserve of hypocrisy, the affected demeanour either of a prude or a coquette, that we admire; but it is the simple, graceful, natural modesty of a woman, whose mind is innocent. With this belief impressed upon her heart, do you think, my dear friend, that she who can reflect and reason would take the means to disgust where she wishes to please? or that she would incur contempt, when she knows how to secure esteem? — Do you think that she will employ artifice to entangle some heedless heart, when she knows that every heart which can be so won is not worth the winning? –

She will not look upon our sex either as dupes or tyrants; she will be aware of the important difference between evanescent passion, and that affection founded upon mutual esteem, which forms the permanent happiness of life.

I am not apprehensive, my dear sir, that Cupid should be scared by the helmet of Minerva; he has conquered his idle fears, and has been familiarized to Minerva and the Muses:

> And now of power his darts are found,
> Twice ten thousand times to wound.[49]

That the power of beauty over the human heart is infinitely increased by the associated ideas of virtue and intellectual excellence has been long acknowledged. – A set of features, however regular, inspire but little admiration or enthusiasm, unless they be irradiated by that sunshine of the soul which creates beauty. The expression of intelligent benevolence renders even homely features and cheeks of sorry grain[50] agreeable; and it has been observed, that the most lasting attachments have not always been excited by the most beautiful of the sex. As men have become more cultivated, they have attended more to the expression of amiable and estimable qualities in the female countenance; and in all probability the taste for this species of beauty will increase amongst the good and wise. When agreeable qualities are connected with the view of any particular form, we learn to love that form, though it may have no other merit. Women who have no pretensions to Grecian beauty may, if their countenances are expressive of good temper and good sense, have some chance of pleasing men of cultivated minds. – In an excellent Review of Gillier's *Essays on the Causes of the Perfection of Antique Sculpture*, which I have just seen, it is observed, that our exclusive admiration of the physiognomy of the Greeks arises from prejudice, since the Grecian countenance cannot be necessarily associated with any of the perfections which now distinguish accomplished or excellent men.[51] This remark in a popular periodical work shows that the public mind is not bigoted in matters of taste, and that the standard is no longer supposed to be fixed by the voice of ancient authority.

The changes that are made in the opinions of our sex as to female beauty, according to the different situations in which women are placed, and the different qualities on which we fix the idea of their excellence, are curious and striking. Ask a northern Indian, says a traveller who has lately visited them, ask a northern Indian what is beauty? and he will answer, a broad flat face, small eyes, high cheek bones, three or four broad black lines across each cheek, a low forehead, a large broad chin, a clumsy hook nose, &c. These beauties are greatly heightened, or at least rendered more valuable, when the possessor is capable of dressing all kinds of skins, converting them into the different parts of their clothing, and able to carry eight or ten stone in summer, or haul a much greater weight in winter. – Prince Matanabbee, adds this author, prided himself much upon the height and strength of his wives, and would frequently say, few women could carry or haul heavier loads.[52] If, some years ago, you had asked a Frenchman what he meant by beauty, he would have talked to you of *l'air piquant, l'air spirituel, l'air noble, l'air comme il faut*, and he would have referred ultimately that *je ne sçais quoi*,[53] for which Parisian belles were formerly celebrated. – French women mixed much in company, the charms of what they called *esprit* were admired in conversation, and the *petit minois* denoting lively wit and coquetry became fashionable in France, whilst gallantry and a taste for the pleasures of *society* prevailed. The countenance expressive of sober sense and modest reserve continues to be the taste of the English, who wisely prefer the pleasures of domestic life. – Domestic life should, however, be enlivened and embellished with all the wit and vivacity and politeness for which French women were once admired, without admitting any of their vices or follies. The more men of literature and polished manners desire to spend their time in their own families, the more they must wish that their wives and daughters may have tastes and habits similar to their own. If they can meet with conversation suited to their taste at home, they will not be driven to clubs for companions; they will invite the men of wit and science of their acquaintance to their own houses, instead of appointing some place of meeting from which ladies are to be excluded. This mixture of the talents and knowledge of both sexes must be advantageous to the interests of society, by increasing domestic happiness. – Private *virtues* are public benefits: if each bee were content in his cell, there could be no grumbling hive; and if each cell were complete, the whole fabric must be perfect.[54]

When you asserted, my dear sir, that learned men usually prefer for their wives, women rather below than above the standard of mental mediocrity, you forgot many instances strongly in contradiction of this opinion. – Since I began this letter, I met with the following pathetic passage, which I cannot forbear transcribing:

"The greatest part of the observations contained in the foregoing pages were derived from a lady, who is now beyond the reach of being affected by any thing in this sublunary world. Her beneficence of disposition induced her never to overlook any fact or circumstance that fell within the sphere of her observation, which promised to be in any respect beneficial to her fellow-creatures. To her gentle influence the public are indebted, if they be indeed indebted at all, for whatever useful hints may at any time have dropped from my pen. A being, she thought, who must depend so much as man does on the assistance of others, owes, as a debt to his fellow-creatures, the communication of the little useful knowledge that chance may have thrown in his way. Such has been my constant aim; such were the views of the wife of my bosom, the friend of my heart, who supported and assisted me in all my pursuits. – I now feel a melancholy satisfaction in contemplating those objects she once delighted to elucidate."[55]

Dr Gregory, Haller, and Lord Lyttleton,[56] have, in the language of affection, poetry, and truth, described the pleasures which men of science and literature enjoy in an union with women who can sympathize in all their thoughts and feelings, who can converse with them as equals, and live with them as friends; who can assist them in the important and delightful duty of educating their children; who can make their family their most agreeable society, and their home the attractive centre of happiness.

Can women of uncultivated understandings make such wives or such mothers?

LETTERS OF
JULIA AND CAROLINE

No penance can absolve their guilty fame,
Nor tears, that wash out guilt, can wash out shame. — *Prior*

LETTER I

Julia to Caroline

In vain, dear Caroline, you urge me to *think*; I profess only to *feel*.

"*Reflect upon my own feelings*! Analyse my notions of happiness! explain to you my system!" — My system! But I have no system: *that* is the very difference between us. My notions of happiness cannot be resolved into simple, fixed principles. Nor dare I even attempt to analyse them; the subtle essence would escape in the process: just punishment to the alchymist in morality!

You, Caroline, are of a more sedate, contemplative character. Philosophy becomes the rigid mistress of your life, enchanting enthusiasm the companion of mine. Suppose she lead me now and then in pursuit of a meteor; am not I happy in the chase? When one illusion vanishes, another shall appear, and, still leading me forward towards an horizon that retreats as I advance, the happy prospect of futurity shall vanish only with my existence.

"Reflect upon my feelings!" — Dear Caroline, is it not enough that I do feel? — All that I dread is that *apathy* which philosophers call tranquillity. You tell me that by continually *indulging*, I shall weaken my natural sensibility; — are not all the faculties of the soul improved, refined by exercise? and why shall *this* be excepted from the general law?

But I must not, you tell me, indulge my taste for romance and poetry, lest I waste that sympathy on *fiction* which *reality* so much better deserves. My dear friend, let us cherish the precious propensity to pity! no matter what the object; sympathy with fiction or reality arises from the same disposition.

When the sigh of compassion rises in my bosom, when the spontaneous tear starts from my eye, what frigid moralist shall "stop the genial current of the soul"? shall say to the tide of passion, *So far shalt thou go, and no farther*? – Shall man presume to circumscribe that which Providence has left unbounded?

But oh, Caroline! if our feelings as well as our days are numbered; if, by the immutable law of nature, apathy be the sleep of passion, and languor the necessary consequence of exertion; if indeed the pleasures of life are so ill proportioned to its duration, oh, may that duration be shortened to me! – Kind Heaven, let not my soul die before my body!

Yes, if at this instant my guardian genius were to appear before me, and offering me the choice of my future destiny; on the one hand, the even temper, the poised judgment, the stoical serenity of philosophy; on the other, the eager genius, the exquisite sensibility of enthusiasm: if the genius said to me, "Choose" – the lot of the one is great pleasure, and great pain – great virtues, and great defects – ardent hope, and severe disappointment – ecstasy, and despair: – the lot of the other is calm happiness unmixed with violent grief – virtue without heroism – respect without admiration – and a length of life, in which to every moment is allotted its proper portion of felicity: –Gracious genius! I should exclaim, if half my existence must be the sacrifice, take it; *enthusiasm is my choice*.

Such, my dear friend, would be my choice were I a man; as a woman, how much more readily should I determine!

What has woman to do with philosophy? The graces flourish not under her empire; a woman's part in life is to please, and Providence has assigned to her *success*, all the pride and pleasure of her being.

Then leave us our weakness, leave us our follies; they are our best arms: –

> Leave us to trifle with more grace and ease,
> Whom folly pleases and whose follies please.

The moment grave sense and solid merit appear, adieu the bewitching caprice, the "*lively nonsense*", the exquisite, yet childish susceptibility which charms, interests, captivates. – Believe me, our *amiable defects* win more than our noblest virtues. Love requires sympathy, and sympathy is seldom connected with a sense of superiority. I envy none their "*painful pre-eminence.*"[57] Alas! whether it be deformity or excellence which makes us say with Richard the Third,

> I am myself alone!

it comes to much the same thing. Then let us, Caroline, content ourselves to gain in love, what we lose in esteem.

Man is to be held only by the *slightest* chains; with the idea that he can break them at pleasure, he submits to them in sport; but his pride revolts against the power to which his *reason* tells him he ought to submit. What then can woman gain by reason? Can she prove by argument that she is amiable? or demonstrate that she is an angel?

Vain was the industry of the artist, who, to produce the image of perfect beauty, selected from the fairest faces their most faultless features. Equally vain must be the efforts of the philosopher, who would excite the idea of mental perfection, by combining an assemblage of party-coloured virtues.

Such, I had almost said, is my *system*, but I mean my *sentiments*. I am not accurate enough to compose a *system*. After all, how vain are systems, and theories, and reasonings!

We may *declaim*, but what do we really know? All is uncertainty – human prudence does nothing – fortune every thing: I leave every thing therefore to fortune; *you* leave nothing. Such is the difference between us, – and which shall be the happiest, time alone can decide.

Farewell, dear Caroline; I love you better than I thought I could love a philosopher.

Your ever affectionate

JULIA.

LETTER II

Caroline's answer to Julia

At the hazard of ceasing to be "*charming*", "*interesting*", "*captivating*", I must, dear Julia, venture to reason with you, to examine your favourite doctrine of "*amiable defects*", and, if possible, to dissipate that unjust dread of perfection which you seem to have continually before your eyes.

It is the sole object of a woman's life, you say, to *please*. Her amiable defects *please* more than her noblest virtues, her follies more than her wisdom, her caprice more than her temper, and *something*, a nameless something, which no art can imitate and no science can teach, more than all.

Art, you say, spoils the graces, and corrupts the heart of woman; and at best can produce only a cold model of perfection; which though perhaps strictly conformable to *rule*, can never touch the soul, or please the unprejudiced taste, like one simple stroke of genuine nature.

I have often observed, dear Julia, that an inaccurate use of words produces such a strange confusion in all reasoning, that in the heat of debate, the combatants, unable to distinguish their friends from their foes, fall promiscuously on both. A skilful disputant knows well how to take advantage of this confusion, and sometimes endeavours to create it. I do not know whether I am to suspect you of such a design; but I must guard against it.

You have with great address availed yourself of the *two* ideas connected with the word *art*: first, as opposed to simplicity, it implies artifice; and next, as opposed to ignorance, it comprehends all the improvements of science, which leading us to search for general causes, rewards us with a dominion over their dependent effects: – that which instructs how to pursue the objects which we may have in view with the greatest probability of success. All men who act from general principles are so far philosophers. Their objects may be, when attained, insufficient to their happiness, or they may not previously have known all the necessary means to obtain them: but they must not therefore complain, if they do not meet with success which they have no reason to expect.

Parrhasius, in collecting the most admired excellences from various models, to produce perfection, concluded, from general principles that mankind would be pleased again with what had once excited their admiration. – So far he was a philosopher: but he was disappointed of success: – yes, for he was ignorant of the cause necessary to produce it. The separate features might be perfect, but they were unsuited to each other, and in their forced union he could not give to the whole countenance symmetry and an appropriate expression.

There was, as you say, a *something* wanting, which his science had not taught him. He should then have set himself to examine what that *something* was, and how it was to be obtained. His want of success arose from the *insufficiency*, not the *fallacy*, of theory. Your object, dear Julia, we will suppose is "to please". If general observation and experience have taught you, that slight accomplishments and a trivial character succeed more certainly in obtaining this end, than higher worth and sense, you act from principle in rejecting the one and aiming at the other. You have discovered, or think you have discovered, the secret causes which produce the desired effect, and you employ them. Do not call this *instinct* or *nature*; this also, though you scorn it, is *philosophy*.

But when you come soberly to reflect, you have a feeling in your mind, that reason and cool judgment disapprove of the part you are acting.

Let us, however, distinguish between disapprobation of the *object*, and the means.

Averse as enthusiasm is from the retrograde motion of analysis, let me, my dear friend, lead you one step backward.

Why do you wish to please? I except at present from the question, the desire to please, arising from a passion which requires a reciprocal return. Confined as *this* wish must be in a woman's heart to one object alone, when you say, Julia *that the admiration of others* will be absolutely necessary to your happiness, I must suppose you mean to express only a *general* desire to please?

Then under this limitation – let me ask you again, why do you wish to please?

Do not let a word stop you. The word *vanity* conveys to us a disagreeable idea. There seems something *selfish* in the sentiment – that all the pleasure we feel in pleasing others arises from the gratification it affords to our own *vanity*.

We refine, and explain, and never can bring ourselves fairly to make a confession, which we are sensible must lower us in the opinion of others, and consequently mortify the very *vanity* we would conceal. So strangely then do we deceive ourselves as to deny the existence of a motive, which at the instant prompts the denial. But let us, dear Julia, exchange the word *vanity* for a less odious word, self-complacency; let us acknowledge that we wish to please, because the success raises our self-complacency. If you ask why raising our self-approbation gives us pleasure, I must answer, that I do not know. Yet I see and feel that it does; I observe that the voice of numbers is capable of raising the highest transport or the most fatal despair. The eye of man seems to possess a fascinating power over his fellow-creatures, to raise the blush of shame, or the glow of pride.

I look around me, and I see riches, titles, dignities, pursued with such eagerness by thousands, only as the signs of distinction. Nay, are not all these things sacrificed the moment they cease to be distinctions? The moment the prize of glory is to be won by other means, do not millions sacrifice their fortunes, their peace, their health, their lives, for *fame*? Then amongst the highest pleasures of human beings I must place self-approbation. With this belief, let us endeavour to secure it in the greatest extent, and to the longest duration.

Then Julia, the wish to please becomes only a secondary motive, subordinate to the desire I have to secure my own self-complacency. We will examine how far they are connected.

In reflecting upon my own mind, I observe that I am flattered by the opinion of others, in proportion to the opinion I have previously formed of their judgment; or I perceive that the opinion of numbers, merely as numbers, has power to give me great pleasure or great pain. I would unite both these pleasures if

I could, but in general I cannot – they are incompatible. The opinion of the vulgar crowd and the enlightened individual, the applause of the highest and the lowest of mankind, cannot be obtained by the same means.

Another question then arises, – whom shall we wish to please? We must choose, and be decided in the choice.

You say that you are proud; I am prouder. – You will be content with indiscriminate admiration – nothing will content me but what is *select*. As long as I have the use of my reason – as long as my heart can feel the delightful sense of a "well-earned praise", I will fix my eye on the highest pitch of excellence, and steadily endeavour to attain it.

Conscious of her worth, and daring to assert it, I would have a woman early in life know that she is capable of filling the heart of a man of sense and merit; that she is worthy to be his companion and friend. With all the energy of her soul, with all the powers of her understanding, I would have a woman endeavour to please those whom she esteems and loves.

She runs a risk, you will say, of never meeting her equal. Hearts and understandings of a superior order are seldom met with in the world; or when met with, it may not be a particular good fortune to win them. – True; but if ever she *wins*, she will *keep* them; and the prize appears to me well worth the pains and difficulty of attaining.

I, Julia, admire and feel enthusiasm; but I would have philosophy directed to the highest objects. I dread apathy as much as you can; and I would endeavour to prevent it, not by sacrificing half my existence, but by enjoying the whole with moderation.

You ask, why exercise does not increase sensibility, and why sympathy with imaginary distress will not also increase the disposition to sympathize with what is real? – Because pity should, I think, always be associated with the active desire to relieve. If it be suffered to become a *passive sensation*, it is a *useless weakness*, not a virtue. The species of reading you speak of must be hurtful, even in this respect, to the mind, as it indulges all the luxury of woe in sympathy with fictitious distress, without requiring the exertion which reality demands: besides, universal experience proves to us that habit, so far from increasing sensibility, absolutely destroys it, by familiarizing it with objects of compassion.

Let me, my dear friend, appeal even to your own experience in the very instance you mention. Is there any pathetic writer in the world who could move you as much at the "twentieth reading as at the first"?[59] Speak naturally, and at the third or fourth reading, you would probably say, It is very pathetic, but I have read it before – I liked it better the first time; that is to say, it *did* touch me once – I know it *ought* to touch me now, but it *does not*. Beware of this! Do not let life become *as tedious as a twice-told tale.*[60]

Farewell, dear Julia: this is the answer of fact against eloquence, philosophy against enthusiasm. You appeal from my understanding to my heart – I appeal from the heart to the understanding of my judge; and ten years hence the decision perhaps will be in my favour.

Yours sincerely,
CAROLINE.

LETTER III

Caroline to Julia
On her intended marriage

Indeed, my dear Julia, I hardly know how to venture to give you my advice upon a subject which ought to depend so much upon your own taste and feelings. My opinion and my wishes I could readily tell you: the idea of seeing you united and attached to my brother is certainly the most agreeable to me; but I am to divest myself of the partiality of a sister, and to consider my brother and Lord V— as equal candidates for your preference – equal, I mean, in your regard; for you say that "Your heart is not yet decided in its choice. – If that oracle would declare itself in intelligible terms, you would not hesitate a moment to obey its dictates." But, my dear Julia, is there not another, a *safer*, I do not say a *better* oracle, to be consulted – your reason? Whilst the "doubtful beam still nods from side to side", you may with a steady hand weigh your own motives, and determine what things will be essential to your happiness, and what *price* you will pay for them; for

> Each pleasure has its *price*; and they who pay
> Too much of pain, but squander life away.

Do me the justice to believe that I do not quote these lines of Dryden as being the finest poetry he ever wrote; for poets, you know, as Waller wittily observed, never succeed so well in truth as in fiction.[61]

Since we cannot in life expect to realize all our wishes, we must distinguish those which claim the rank of wants. We must separate the fanciful from the real, or at least make the one subservient to the other.

It is of the utmost importance to you, more particularly, to take every precaution before you decide for life, because disappointment and restraint afterwards would be insupportable to your temper.

You have often declared to me, my dear friend, that your love of poetry, and of all the refinements of literary and romantic pursuits, is so intimately "interwoven in your mind, that nothing could separate them, without destroying the whole fabric".

Your tastes, you say, are fixed; if they are so, you must be doubly careful to ensure their gratification. If you cannot make *them* subservient to external circumstances, you should certainly, if it be in your power, choose a situation in which circumstances will be subservient to them. If you are convinced that you could not adopt the tastes of another, it will be absolutely necessary for your happiness to live with one whose tastes are similar to your own.

The belief in that sympathy of souls, which the poets suppose declares itself between two people at first sight, is perhaps as absurd as the late fashionable belief in animal magnetism:[62] but there is a sympathy which, if it be not the foundation, may be called the cement of affection. Two people could not, I should think, retain any lasting affection for each other, without a mutual sympathy in taste and in their diurnal occupations and domestic pleasures. This, you will allow, my dear Julia, even in a fuller extent than I do. Now, my brother's tastes, character, and habits of life, are so very different from Lord V—'s, that I scarcely know how you can compare them; at least before you can decide which of the two would make you the happiest in life, you must determine what kind of life you may wish to lead; for my brother, though he might make you very happy in domestic life, would not make the Countess of V— happy; nor would Lord V— make Mrs. Percy happy. They must be two different women, with different habits, and different wishes; so that you must divide yourself, my dear Julia, like Araspes, into two selves; I do not say into a bad and a good self; choose some other epithets to distinguish them, but distinct they must be: so let them now declare and decide their pretensions; and let the victor have not only the honours of a triumph, but all the prerogatives of victory. Let the subdued be subdued for life – let the victor take every precaution which policy can dictate, to prevent the possibility of future contests with the vanquished.

But without talking poetry to you, my dear friend, let me seriously recommend it to you to examine your own mind carefully; and if you find that public diversions and public admiration, dissipation, and all the pleasures of riches and high rank, are really and truly essential to your happiness, direct your choice accordingly. Marry Lord V—: he has a large fortune, extensive connexions, and an exalted station; his own taste for show and expense, his family pride, and personal vanity, will all tend to the end you propose. Your house, table, equipages, may be all in the highest style of magnificence. Lord V—'s easiness of temper, and fondness for you, will readily give you that entire ascendancy over his pleasures, which your abilities give you over his understanding. He will not control your wishes; you may gratify them to the utmost bounds of his fortune, and perhaps beyond those bounds; you may have entire command at home and abroad. If these are your objects, Julia, take them; they are in your power. But remember, you must take them with their necessary concomitants – the restraints upon your time, upon the choice of your friends and your company, which high life imposes; the *ennui* subsequent to dissipation; the mortifications of rivalship in beauty, wit, rank, and magnificence; the trouble of managing a large fortune, and the chance of involving your affairs and your family in difficulty and distress; these and a thousand more evils you must submit to. You must renounce all the pleasures of the heart and of the imagination; you must give up the idea of cultivating literary taste; you must not expect from your husband friendship and confidence, or any of the delicacies of affection: – you govern him, he cannot therefore be your equal; you may be a fond mother, but you cannot educate your children; you will neither have the time nor the power to do it; you must trust them to a governess. In the selection of your friends, and in the enjoyment of their company and conversation you will be still more restrained: in short, you must give up the pleasures of domestic life; for that is not in this case the life you have chosen. But you will exclaim against me for supposing you capable of making such a choice – such sacrifices! – I am sure, *next to my brother*, I am the last person in the world who would wish you to make them.

You have another choice, my dear Julia: domestic life is offered to you by one who has every wish and every power to make it agreeable to you; by one whose tastes resemble your own; who would be a judge and a fond admirer of all your perfections. You would have perpetual motives to cultivate every talent, and to exert every power of pleasing for his sake – for *his* sake, whose penetration no improvement would escape, and whose affection would be susceptible of every proof of yours. Am I drawing too flattering a picture? – A sister's hand may draw a partial likeness, but still it will be a likeness. At all events, my dear Julia, you would be certain of the mode of life you would lead with my brother. The regulation of your time and occupations would be your own. In the education of your family, you would meet with no interruptions or restraint. You would have no governess to counteract, no strangers to intrude; you might follow your own judgment, or yield to the judgment of one who would never require you to submit to his opinion, but to his reasons.

All the pleasures of friendship you would enjoy in your own family in the highest perfection, and you would have for your sister the friend of your infancy,

CAROLINE.

LETTER IV

Caroline to Lady V—
Upon her intended separation from her husband

You need not fear, my dear Lady V—, that I should triumph in the accomplishment of my prophecies; or that I should reproach you for having preferred your own opinion to my advice. Believe me, my dear Julia, I am your friend, nor would the name of sister have increased my friendship.

Five years have made then so great a change in your feelings and views of life, that a few days ago, when my letter to you on your marriage accidentally fell into your hands, "*you were struck with a species of astonishment at your choice, and you burst into tears in an agony of despair, on reading the wretched doom foretold to the wife of Lord V—. A doom,*" you add, "*which I feel hourly accomplishing, and which I see no possibility of averting, but by a separation from a husband, with whom, I now think, it was madness to unite myself.*" Your opinion I must already know upon this subject, "*as the same arguments which should have prevented me from making such a choice, ought now to determine me to abjure it.*"

You say, dear Julia, that my letter struck you with despair. – Despair is either madness or folly; it obtains, it deserves nothing from mankind but pity; and pity, though it be akin to love, has yet a secret affinity to contempt. In strong minds, despair is an acute disease; the prelude to great exertion. In weak minds, it is a chronic distemper, followed by incurable indolence. Let the crisis be favourable, and resume your wonted energy. Instead of suffering the imagination to dwell with unavailing sorrow on the past, let us turn our attention towards the future. When an evil is irremediable, let us acknowledge it to be such, and bear it: — there is no power to which we submit so certainly as to necessity. With our hopes, our wishes cease. Imagination has a contracting, as well as an expansive faculty. The prisoner, who, deprived of all that we conceive to constitute the pleasures of life, could interest or occupy himself with the labours of a spider, was certainly a philosopher. He enjoyed all the means of happiness that were left in his power.

I know, my dear Lady V—, that words have little effect over grief; and I do not, I assure you, mean to insult you with the parade of stoic philosophy. But consider, your error is not perhaps so great as you imagine. Certainly, they who at the beginning of life can with a steady eye look through the long perspective of distant years, who can in one view comprise all the different objects of happiness and misery, who can compare accurately, and justly estimate their respective degrees of importance; and who, after having formed such a calculation, are capable of acting uniformly, in consequence of their own conviction, are the *wisest*, and, as far as prudence can influence our fortune, the *happiest* of human beings. Next to this favoured class are those who can perceive and repair their own errors; who can stop at any given period to take a new view of life. If unfortunate circumstances have denied you a place in the first rank, you may, dear Julia, secure yourself a station in the second. Is not the conduct of a woman, after her marriage, of infinitely more importance than her previous choice, whatever it may have been? Then now consider what yours should be.

You say that it is easier to *break* a chain than to *stretch* it; but remember that when broken, your part of the chain, Julia, will still remain with you, and fetter and disgrace you through life. Why should a woman be so circumspect in her choice? Is it not because when once made she must abide by it? "She sets her life upon the cast, and she must stand the hazard of the die."[63] From domestic uneasiness a man has a thousand resources: in middling life, the tavern, in high life, the gaming-table, suspends the anxiety of thought. Dissipation, ambition, business, the occupation of a profession, change of place, change of company, afford him agreeable and honourable relief from domestic chagrin. If his home become tiresome, he leaves it; if his wife become disagreeable to him, he leaves her, and in leaving her loses *only* a wife. But what resource has a woman? – Precluded from all the occupations common to the other sex, she loses even those peculiar to her own. She has no remedy, from the company of a man she dislikes, but a separation; and this remedy, desperate as it is, is allowed only to a certain class of women in society; to those whose fortune affords them the means of subsistence, and whose friends have secured to them a separate maintenance. A peeress then, probably, can leave her husband if she wish it; a peasant's wife cannot; she depends upon the character and privileges of a wife for actual subsistence. Her domestic care, if not her affection, is secured to her husband; and it is just that it should. He sacrifices his liberty, his labour, his ingenuity, his time, for the support and protection of his wife; and in proportion to his protection is his power.

In higher life, where the sacrifices of both parties in the original union are more equal, the evils of a separation are more nearly balanced. But even here, the wife who has hazarded least, suffers the most by the dissolution of the partnership; she loses a great part of her fortune, and of the conveniences and luxuries of life. She loses her home, her rank in society. She loses both the repellant and the attractive power of a mistress of a family. "Her occupation is gone."[64] She becomes a wanderer. Whilst her youth and beauty last, she may enjoy that species of delirium, caused by public admiration; fortunate if habit does not destroy the power of this charm, before the season of its duration expire. It was said to be the wish of a celebrated modern beauty, "that she might not survive her nine-and-twentieth birth-day". I have often heard this wish quoted for its extravagance; but I always admired it for its good sense. The lady foresaw the inevitable doom of her declining years. Her apprehensions for the future embittered even her enjoyment of the present; and she had resolution enough to offer to take "a bond of fate",[65] to sacrifice one-half of her life, to secure the pleasure of the other.

But, dear Lady V—, probably this wish was made at some distance from the destined period of its accomplishment. On the eve of her nine-and-twentieth birth-day, the lady perhaps might have felt inclined to retract her prayer. At least we should provide for the cowardice which might seize the female mind at such an instant. Even the most wretched life has power to attach us; none can be more wretched than the old age of a dissipated beauty: – unless, Lady V—, it be that of a woman, who, to all her evils has the addition of remorse, for having abjured her duties and abandoned her family. Such is the situation of a woman who separates from her husband. Reduced to go the same insipid round of public amusements, yet more restrained than an unmarried beauty in youth, yet more miserable in age, the superiority of her genius and the sensibility of her heart become her greatest evils. She, indeed, must pray for indifference. Avoided by all her family connexions, hated and despised where she might have been loved and respected, solitary in the midst of society, she feels herself deserted at the time of life when she most wants social comfort and assistance.

Dear Julia, whilst it is yet in your power secure to yourself a happier fate; retire to the bosom of your own family; prepare for yourself a new society; perform the duties, and you shall soon enjoy the pleasures of domestic life; educate your children; whilst they are young, it shall be your occupation; as they grow up, it shall be your glory. Let me anticipate your future success, when they shall appear such as you can make them; when the world shall ask "who educated these amiable young women? Who formed their character? Who cultivated the talents of this promising young man? Why does this whole family live together in such perfect union?" With one voice, dear Julia, your children shall name their mother; she who in the bloom of youth checked herself in the career of dissipation, and turned all the ability and energy of her mind to their education.

Such will be your future fame. In the mean time, before you have formed for yourself companions in your own family, you will want a society suited to your taste. "Disgusted as you have been with frivolous company, you say that you wish to draw around you a society of literary and estimable friends, whose conversation and talents shall delight you, and who at the same time that they are excited to display their own abilities, shall be a judge of yours."

But, dear Lady V—, the possibility of your forming such a society must depend on your having a home to receive, a character and consequence in life to invite and attach friends. The opinion of numbers is necessary to excite the ambition of individuals. To be a female Mecænas you must have power to confer favours, as well as judgment to discern merit.[66]

What castles in the air are built by the synthetic wand of imagination, which vanish when exposed to the analysis of reason!

Then, Julia, supposing that Lord V—, as your husband, becomes a negative quantity as to your happiness, yet he will acquire another species of value as the master of your family and the father of your children; as a person who supports your public consequence, and your private self-complacency. Yes, dear Lady V—, he will increase your self-complacency; for do you not think, that when your husband sees his children prosper under your care, his family united under your management – whilst he feels your merit at home, and hears your praises abroad, do you not think he will himself learn to respect and love you? You say that "*he is not a judge of female excellence; that he has no real taste; that vanity is his ruling passion.*" Then if his judgment be dependent on the opinions of others, he will be the more easily led by the public voice, and you will command the suffrages of the public. If he has not taste enough to approve, he will have vanity enough to be proud of you; and a vain man insensibly begins to love that of which he is proud. Why does Lord V— love his buildings, his paintings, his equipages? It is not for their intrinsic value; but because they are means of distinction to him. Let his wife become a greater distinction to him, and on the same principles he will prefer her. Set an example, then, dear Lady V—, of domestic virtue; your talents shall make it admired, your rank shall make it conspicuous. You are ambitious, Julia, you love praise; you have been used to it; you cannot live happily without it.

Praise is a mental luxury, which becomes from habit absolutely necessary to our existence; and in purchasing it we must pay the price set upon it by society. The more curious, the more avaricious we become of this "aerial coin", the more it is our interest to preserve its currency and increase its value. You, my dear Julia, in particular, who have amassed so much of it, should not cry down its price, for your own sake! – Do not then say in a fit of disgust, that "you are grown too wise now to value applause."

If during youth, your appetite for applause was indiscriminate, and indulged to excess, you are now more difficult in your choice, and are become an *epicure* in your *taste* for praise.

Adieu, my dear Julia; I hope still to see you as happy in domestic life as

Your ever affectionate
and sincere friend,
CAROLINE.

LETTER V

Caroline to Lady V—
On her conduct after her separation from her husband

A delicacy, of which I now begin to repent, has of late prevented me from writing to you. I am afraid I shall be abrupt, but it is necessary to be explicit. Your conduct, ever since your separation from your husband, has been anxiously watched from a variety of motives, by his family and your own; – it has been blamed. Reflect upon your own mind, and examine with what justice.

Last summer, when I was with you, I observed a change in your conversation, and the whole turn of your thoughts. I perceived an unusual impatience of restraint; a confusion in your ideas when you began to reason, – an eloquence in your language when you began to declaim, which convinced me that from some secret cause the powers of your reason had been declining, and those of your imagination rapidly increasing; the boundaries of right and wrong seemed to be no longer marked in your mind. Neither the rational hope of happiness, nor a sense of duty governed you; but some unknown, wayward power seemed to have taken possession of your understanding, and to have thrown every thing into confusion. You appeared peculiarly averse to philosophy: let me recall your own words to you; you asked "of what use philosophy could be to beings who had no free will, and how the ideas of just punishment and involuntary crime could be reconciled?"

Your understanding involved itself in metaphysical absurdity. In conversing upon literary subjects one evening, in speaking of the striking difference between the conduct and the understanding of the great Lord Bacon, you said, that "It by no means surprised you; that to an enlarged mind, accustomed to consider the universe as one vast *whole*, the conduct of that little animated atom, that inconsiderable part *self*, must be too insignificant to fix or merit attention.[67] It was nothing," you said, "in the general mass of vice and virtue, happiness and misery." I believe I answered, "that it might be *nothing* compared to the great *whole*, but it was *every thing* to the individual." Such were your opinions in theory; you must know enough of the human heart to perceive their tendency when reduced to practice. Speculative opinions, I know, have little influence over the practice of those who *act* much and think little; but I should conceive their power to be considerable over the conduct of those who have much time for reflection and little necessity for action. In one case the habit of action governs the thoughts upon any sudden emergency; in the other, the thoughts govern the actions. The truth or falsehood then of speculative opinions is of much greater consequence to our sex than to the other; as we live a life of reflection, they of action.

Retrace, then, dear Julia, in your mind the course of your thoughts for some time past; discover the cause of this revolution in your opinions; judge yourself; and remember, that in the *mind* as well as in the body, the highest pitch of disease is often attended with an unconsciousness of its existence. If, then, Lady V—, upon receiving my letter, you should feel averse to this self-examination, or if you should imagine it to be useless, I no longer advise, I command you to quit your present abode; come to me: fly from the danger, and be safe.

Dear Julia, I must assume this peremptory tone: if you are angry, I must disregard your anger; it is the anger of disease, the anger of one who is roused from that sleep which would end in death.

I respect the equality of friendship; but this equality permits, nay requires, the temporary ascendancy I assume. In real friendship, the judgment, the genius, the prudence of each party become the common property of both. Even if they are equals, they may not be so *always*. Those transient fits of passion, to which the best and wisest are liable, may deprive even the superior of the advantage of their reason. She then has still in her friend an *impartial*, though perhaps an inferior judgment; each becomes the guardian of the other, as their mutual safety may require.

Heaven seems to have granted this double chance of virtue and happiness, as the peculiar reward of friendship.

Use it, then, my dear friend; accept the assistance you could so well return. Obey me; I shall judge of you by your resolution at this crisis: on it depends your fate, and my friendship.

Your sincere
and affectionate
CAROLINE.

LETTER VI

Caroline to Lady V—
Just before she went to France

The time is now come, Lady V—, when I must bid you an eternal adieu. With what deep regret, I need not, Julia, I cannot tell you.

I burned your letter the moment I had read it. Your past confidence I never will betray; but I must renounce all future intercourse with you. I am a sister, a wife, a mother; all these connexions forbid me to be longer your friend. In misfortune, in sickness, or in poverty, I never would have forsaken you; but infamy I cannot share. I would have gone, I went, to the brink of the precipice to save you; with all my force I held you back; but in vain. But why do I vindicate my conduct to you now? Accustomed as I have always been to think your approbation necessary to my happiness, I forgot that henceforward your opinion is to be nothing to me, or mine to you.

Oh, Julia! the idea, the certainty, that you must, if you live, be in a few years, in a few months, perhaps, reduced to absolute want, in a foreign country – without a friend – a protector, the fate of women who have fallen from a state as high as yours, the names of L—, of G—, the horror I feel at joining your name to theirs, impels me to make one more attempt to save you.

Companion of my earliest years! friend of my youth! my beloved Julia! by the happy innocent hours we have spent together, by the love you had for me, by the respect you bear to the memory of your mother, by the agony with which your father will hear of the loss of his daughter, by all that has power to touch your mind – I conjure you, I implore you to pause! – Farewell!

CAROLINE.

LETTER VII

Caroline to Lord V—
Written a few months after the date of the preceding letter

MY LORD,
Though I am too sensible that all connexion between my unfortunate friend and her family must for some time have been dissolved, I venture now to address myself to your lordship.

On Wednesday last, about half after six o'clock in the evening, the following note was brought to me. It had been written with such a trembling hand that it was scarcely legible; but I knew the writing too well.

"If you ever loved me, Caroline, read this – do not tear it the moment you see the name of Julia: she has suffered – she is humbled. I left France with the hope of seeing you once more, but now I am so near you, my courage fails, and my heart sinks within me. I have no friend upon earth – I deserve none; yet I cannot help wishing to see, once more before I die, the friend of my youth, to thank her with my last breath.

"But, dear Caroline, if I must not see you, write to me, if possible, one line of consolation.

"Tell me, is my father living – do you know any thing of my children? – I dare not ask for my husband. Adieu! I am so weak that I can scarcely write – I hope I shall soon be no more. Farewell!

"JULIA."

I immediately determined to follow the bearer of this letter. Julia was waiting for my answer at a small inn in a neighbouring village, at a few miles' distance. It was night when I got there: every thing was silent – all the houses were shut up, excepting one, in which we saw two or three lights glimmering through the window – this was the inn: as your lordship may imagine, it was a very miserable place. The mistress of the house seemed to be touched with pity for the stranger: she opened the door of a small room, where she said the poor lady was resting; and retired as I entered.

Upon a low matted seat beside the fire sat Lady V—; she was in black; her knees were crossed, and her white but emaciated arms flung on one side over her lap; her hands were clasped together, and her eyes fixed upon the fire: she seemed neither to hear nor see any thing round her, but, totally absorbed in her own reflections, to have sunk into insensibility. I dreaded to rouse her from this state of torpor; and I believe I stood for some moments motionless: at last I moved softly towards her – she turned her head – started up – a scarlet blush overspread her face – she grew livid again instantly, gave a faint shriek, and sunk senseless into my arms.

When she returned to herself, and found her head lying upon

my shoulder, and heard my voice soothing her with all the expressions of kindness I could think of, she smiled with a look of gratitude, which I never shall forget. Like one who had been long unused to kindness, she seemed ready to pour forth all the fondness of her heart: but, as if recollecting herself better, she immediately checked her feelings – withdrew her hand from mine – thanked me – said she was quite well again – cast down her eyes, and her manner changed from tenderness to timidity. She seemed to think that she had lost all right to sympathy, and received even the common offices of humanity with surprise: her high spirit, I saw, was quite broken.

I think I never felt such sorrow as I did in contemplating Julia at this instant: she who stood before me, sinking under the sense of inferiority, I knew to be my equal – my superior; yet by fatal imprudence, by one rash step, all her great, and good, and amiable qualities were irretrievably lost to the world and to herself.

When I thought that she was a little recovered, I begged of her, if she was not too much fatigued, to let me carry her home. At these words she looked at me with surprise. Her eyes filled with tears; but without making any other reply, she suffered me to draw her arm within mine, and attempted to follow me. I did not know how feeble she was till she began to walk; it was with the utmost difficulty I supported her to the door; and by the assistance of the people of the house she was lifted into the carriage: we went very slowly. When the carriage stopped she was seized with an universal tremor; she started when the man knocked at the door, and seemed to dread its being opened. The appearance of light and the sound of cheerful voices struck her with horror.

I could not myself help being shocked with the contrast between the dreadful situation of my friend, and the happiness of the family to which I was returning.

"Oh!" said she, "what are these voices? – Whither are you taking me? – For Heaven's sake do not let any body see me!"

I assured her that she should go directly to her own apartment, and that no human being should approach her without her express permission.

Alas! it happened at this very moment that all my children came running with the utmost gaiety into the hall to meet us, and the very circumstance which I had been so anxious to prevent happened – little Julia was amongst them. The gaiety of the children suddenly ceased the moment they saw Lady V— coming up the steps – they were struck with her melancholy air and countenance: she, leaning upon my arm, with her eyes fixed upon the ground, let me lead her in, and sunk upon the first chair she came to. I made a sign to the children to retire; but the moment they began to move, Lady V— looked up – saw her daughter – and now for the first time burst into tears. The little girl did not recollect her poor mother till she heard the sound of her voice; and then she threw her arms round her neck, crying, "Is that you, mamma?" – and all the children immediately crowded round and asked, "if this was the same Lady V— who used to play with them"?

It is impossible to describe the effect these simple questions had on Julia: a variety of emotions seemed struggling in her countenance; she rose and made an attempt to break from the children, but could not – she had not strength to support herself. We carried her away and put her to bed; she took no notice of any body, nor did she even seem to know that I was with her: I thought she was insensible, but as I drew the curtains I heard her give a deep sigh.

I left her, and carried away her little girl, who had followed us up stairs and begged to stay with her mother; but I was apprehensive that the sight of her might renew her agitation.

After I was gone, they told me that she was perfectly still, with her eyes closed; and I stayed away some time in hopes that she might sleep: however, about midnight she sent to beg to speak to me: she was very ill – she beckoned to me to sit down by her bedside – every one left the room; and when Julia saw herself alone with me, she took my hand, and in a low but calm voice she said, "I have not many hours to live – my heart is broken – I wished to see you, to thank you whilst it was yet in my power." She pressed my hand to her trembling lips: "Your kindness," added she, "touches me more than all the rest; but how ashamed you must be of such a friend! Oh, Caroline! to die a disgrace to all who ever loved me!"

The tears trickled down her face, and choked her utterance: she wiped them away hastily. "But it is not now a time," said she, "to think of myself – can I see my daughter?" The little girl was asleep: she was awakened, and I brought her to her mother. Julia raised herself in her bed, and summoning up all her strength, "My dearest friend!" said she, putting her child's hand into mine, "when I am gone, be a mother to this child – let her know my whole history, let nothing be concealed from her. Poor girl! you will live to blush at your mother's name." She paused and leaned back: I was going to take the child away, but she held out her arms again for her, and kissed her several times. "Farewell!" said she; "I shall never see you again." The little girl burst into tears. Julia wished to say something more – she raised herself again – at last she uttered these words with energy: – "My love, *be good and happy*"; she then sunk down on the pillow quite exhausted – she never spoke afterwards: I took her hand – it was cold – her pulse scarcely beat – her eyes rolled without meaning – in a few moments she expired.

Painful as it has been to me to recall the circumstances of her death to my imagination, I have given your lordship this exact and detailed account of my unfortunate friend's behaviour in her last moments. Whatever may have been her errors, her soul never became callous from vice. The sense of her own ill conduct, was undoubtedly the immediate cause of her illness, and the remorse which had long preyed upon her mind, at length brought her to the grave –

I have the honour to be,

My lord, &c.

CAROLINE.

Written in 1787.
Published in 1795.

AN ESSAY ON THE NOBLE SCIENCE OF
SELF-JUSTIFICATION

"For which an eloquence that aims *to vex*,
  With native tropes of anger arms the *sex*." – *Parnell* [68]

Endowed as the fair sex indisputably are, with a natural genius for the invaluable art of self-justification, it may not be displeasing to them to see its rising perfection evinced by an attempt to reduce it to a science. Possessed, as are all the fair daughters of Eve, of an hereditary propensity, transmitted to them undiminished through succeeding generations, to be "soon moved with slightest touch of blame"; very little precept and practice will confirm them in the habit, and instruct them in all the maxims of self-justification.

Candid pupil, you will readily accede to my first and fundamental axiom – that a lady can do no wrong.

But simple as this maxim may appear, and suited to the level of the meanest capacity, the talent of applying it on all the important, but more especially on all the most trivial, occurrences of domestic life, so as to secure private peace and public dominion, has hitherto been monopolized by the female adepts in the art of self-justification.

Excuse me for insinuating by this expression, that there may yet be amongst you some novices. To these, if any such, I principally address myself.

And now, lest fired by ambition you lose all by aiming at too much, let me explain and limit my first principle, "That you can do no wrong." You must be aware that real perfection is beyond the reach of mortals, nor would I have you aim at it; indeed it is not in any degree necessary to our purpose. You have heard of the established belief in the infallibility of the sovereign pontiff, which prevailed not many centuries ago: [69] – if man was allowed to be infallible, I see no reason why the same privilege should not be extended to woman; – but times have changed; and since the happy age of credulity is past, leave the opinions of men to their natural perversity – their actions are the best test of their faith. Instead then of a belief in your infallibility, endeavour to enforce implicit submission to your authority. This will give you infinitely less trouble, and will answer your purpose as well.

Right and wrong, if we go to the foundation of things, are, as casuists tell us, really words of very dubious signification,[70] perpetually varying with custom and fashion, and to be adjusted ultimately by no other standards but opinion and force. Obtain power, then, by all means: power is the law of man; make it yours.

But to return from a frivolous disquisition about right, let me teach you the art of defending the wrong. After having thus pointed out to you the glorious end of your labours, I must now instruct you in the equally glorious means.

For the advantage of my subject I address myself chiefly to married ladies; but those who have not as yet the good fortune to have that common enemy, a husband, to combat, may in the mean time practise my precepts upon their fathers, brothers, and female friends; with caution, however, lest by discovering their arms too soon, they preclude themselves from the power of using them to the fullest advantage hereafter. I therefore recommend it to them to prefer, with a philosophical moderation, the future to the present.

Timid brides, you have, probably, hitherto been addressed as angels. Prepare for the time when you shall again become mortal. Take the alarm at the first approach of blame; at the first hint of a discovery that you are any thing less than infallible: – contradict, debate, justify, recriminate, rage, weep, swoon, do any thing but yield to conviction.

I take it for granted that you have already acquired sufficient command of voice; you need not study its compass; going beyond its pitch has a peculiarly happy effect upon some occasions. But are you voluble enough to drown all sense in a torrent of words? Can you be loud enough to overpower the voice of all who shall attempt to interrupt or contradict you? Are you mistress of the petulant, the peevish, and the sullen tone? Have you practised the sharpness which provokes retort, and the continual monotony which by setting your adversary to sleep effectually precludes reply? an event which is always to be considered as decisive of the victory, or at least as reducing it to a drawn battle: – you and Somnus divide the prize.[71]

Thus prepared for an engagement, you will next, if you have not already done it, study the weak part of the character of your enemy – your husband, I mean: if he be a man of high spirit, jealous of command and impatient of control, one who decides for himself, and who is little troubled with the insanity of minding what the world says of him, you must proceed with extreme circumspection; you must not dare to provoke the combined forces of the enemy to a regular engagement, but harass him with perpetual petty skirmishes: in these, though you gain little at a time, you will gradually weary the patience, and break the spirit of your opponent. If he be a man of spirit, he must also be generous; and what man of generosity will contend for trifles with a woman who submits to him in all affairs of consequence, who is in his power, who is weak, and who loves him?

"Can superior with inferior power contend?" No; the spirit of a lion is not to be roused by the teasing of an insect.

But such a man as I have described, besides being as generous as he is brave, will probably be of an active temper: then you have an inestimable advantage; for he will set a high value upon a thing for which you have none – time; he will acknowledge the force of your arguments merely from a dread of their length; he will yield to you in trifles, particularly in trifles which do not militate against his authority; not out of regard for you, but for his time; for what man can prevail upon himself to debate three hours about what could be as well decided in three minutes?

Lest amongst infinite variety the difficulty of immediate selection should at first perplex you, let me point out, that matters of *taste* will afford you, of all others, the most ample and incessant subjects of debate. Here you have no criterion to appeal to. Upon the same principle, next to matters of taste, points of opinion will afford the most constant exercise to your talents. Here you will have an opportunity of citing the opinions of all the living and dead you have ever known, besides the dear privilege of repeating continually: – "Nay, you must allow *that*." Or, "You can't deny *this*, for it's the universal opinion – every body says so! every body thinks so! I wonder to hear you express such an opinion! Nobody but yourself is of that way of thinking!" with innumerable other phrases, with which a slight attention to polite conversation will furnish you. This mode of opposing authority to argument, and assertion to proof, is of such universal utility, that I pray you to practise it.

If the point in dispute be some opinion relative to your character or disposition, allow in general, that "you are sure you have a great many faults"; but to every specific charge reply, "Well, I am sure I don't know, but I did not think *that* was one of my faults! nobody ever accused me of that before! Nay, I was always remarkable for the contrary; at least before I was acquainted with you, sir: in my own family I was always remarkable for the contrary: ask any of my own friends; ask any of them; they must know me best."

But if, instead of attacking the material parts of your character, your husband should merely presume to advert to your manners, to some slight personal habit which might be made more agreeable to him; prove, in the first place, that it is his fault that it is not agreeable to him; ask which is most to blame, "she who ceases to please, or he who ceases to be pleased"[72] – His eyes are changed, or opened. But it may perhaps have been a matter almost of indifference to him, till you undertook its defence; then make it of consequence by rising in eagerness, in proportion to the insignificance of your object; if he can draw consequences, this will be an excellent lesson: if you are so tender of blame in the veriest trifles, how impeachable must you be in matters of importance! As to personal habits, begin by denying that you have any; or in the paradoxical language of Rousseau,[73] declare that the only habit you have is the habit of having none, as all personal habits, if they have been of any long standing, must have become involuntary, the unconscious culprit may assert her innocence without hazarding her veracity.

However, if you happen to be detected in the very fact, and a person cries, "Now, now, you are doing it!" submit, but declare at the same moment – "That it is the very first time in your whole life that you were ever known to be guilty of it; and therefore it can be no habit, and of course nowise reprehensible."

Extend the rage for vindication to all the objects which the most remotely concern you; take even inanimate objects under your protection. Your dress, your furniture, your property, every thing which is or has been yours, defend, and this upon the principles of the soundest philosophy: each of these things all compose a part of your personal merit;[74] all that connected the most distantly with your idea gives pleasure or pain to others, becomes an object of blame or praise, and consequently claims your support or vindication.

In the course of the management of your house, children, family, and affairs, probably some few errors of omission or commission may strike your husband's pervading eye; but these errors, admitting them to be errors, you will never, if you please, allow to be charged to any deficiency in memory, judgment, or activity, on your part.

There are surely people enough around you to divide and share the blame; send it from one to another, till at last, by universal rejection, it is proved to belong to nobody. You will say, however, that facts remain unalterable; and that in some unlucky instance, in the changes and chances of human affairs, you may be proved to have been to blame. Some stubborn evidence may appear against you; still you may prove an alibi, or balance the evidence. There is nothing equal to balancing evidence; doubt is, you know, the most philosophic state of the human mind, and it will be kind of you to keep your husband perpetually in this sceptical state.

Indeed the short method of denying absolutely all blameable facts, I should recommend to pupils as the best; and if in the beginning of their career they may startle at this mode, let them depend upon it that in their future practice it must become perfectly familiar. The nice distinction of simulation and dissimulation depends but on the trick of a syllable; palliation and extenuation are universally allowable in self-defence: prevarication inevitably follows, and falsehood "is but in the next degree".

Yet I would not destroy this nicety of conscience too soon. It may be of use in your first setting out, because you must establish credit; in proportion to your credit will be the value of your future asseverations.

In the mean time, however, argument and debate are allowed to the most rigid moralist. You can never perjure yourself by swearing to a false opinion.

I come now to the art of reasoning: don't be alarmed at the name of reasoning, fair pupils; I will explain to you my meaning.

If, instead of the fiery-tempered being I formerly described, you should fortunately be connected with a man, who, having formed a justly high opinion of your sex, should propose to treat you as his equal, and who in any little dispute which might arise between you, should desire no other arbiter than reason; triumph in his mistaken candour, regularly appeal to the decision of reason at the beginning of every contest, and deny its jurisdiction at the conclusion. I take it for granted that you will be on the wrong side of every question, and indeed, in general, I advise you to choose the wrong side of an argument to defend; whilst you are young in the science, it will afford the best exercise, and, as you improve, the best display of your talents.

If, then, reasonable pupils, you would succeed in argument, attend to the following instructions.

Begin by preventing, if possible, the specific statement of any position, or if reduced to it, use the most *general terms*, and take advantage of the ambiguity which all languages and which most philosophers allow. Above all things, shun definitions; they will prove fatal to you; for two persons of sense and candour, who define their terms, cannot argue long without either convincing, or being convinced, or parting in equal good-humour; to prevent which, go over and over the same ground, wander as wide as possible from the point, but always with a view to return at last precisely to the same spot from which you set out. I should remark to you, that the choice of your weapons is a circumstance much to be attended to: choose always those which your adversary cannot use. If your husband is a man of wit, you will of course undervalue a talent which is never connected with judgment: "for your part, you do not presume to contend with him in wit."

But if he be a sober-minded man, who will go link by link along the chain of an argument, follow him at first, till he grows so intent that he does not perceive whether you follow him or not; then slide back to your own station; and when with perverse patience he has at last reached the last link of the chain, with one electric shock of wit make him quit his hold, and strike him to the ground in an instant. Depend upon the sympathy of the spectators, for to one who can understand *reason*, you will find ten who admire *wit*.

But if you should not be blessed with "a ready wit", if demonstration should in the mean time stare you in the face, do not be in the least alarmed — anticipate the blow. Whilst you have it yet in your power, rise with becoming magnanimity, and cry, "I give it up! I give it up! La! let us say no more about it; I do so hate disputing about trifles. I give it up!" Before an explanation on the word trifle can take place, quit the room with flying colours.

If you are a woman of sentiment and eloquence, you have advantages of which I scarcely need apprise you. From the understanding of a man, you have always an appeal to his heart, or, if not, to his affection, to his weakness. If you have the good fortune to be married to a weak man, always choose the moment to argue with him when you have a full audience. Trust to the sublime power of numbers; it will be of use even to excite your own enthusiasm in debate; then as the scene advances, talk of his cruelty, and your sensibility, and sink with "becoming woe" into the pathos of injured innocence.

Besides the heart and the weakness of your opponent, you have still another chance, in ruffling his temper; which, in the course of a long conversation, you will have a fair opportunity of trying; and if – for philosophers will sometimes grow warm in the defence of truth – if he should grow absolutely angry, you will in the same proportion grow calm, and wonder at his rage, though you well know it has been created by your own provocation. The by-standers, seeing anger without any adequate cause, will all be of your side.

Nothing provokes an irascible man, interested in debate, and possessed of an opinion of his own eloquence, so much as to see the attention of his hearers go from him: you will then, when he flatters himself that he has just fixed your eye with his *very best* argument, suddenly grow absent: – your house affairs must call you hence – or you have directions to give to your children – or the room is too hot, or too cold – the window must be opened – or door shut – or the candle wants snuffing. Nay, without these interruptions, the simple motion of your eye may provoke a speaker; a butterfly, or the figure in a carpet may engage your attention in preference to him; or if these objects be absent, the simply averting your eye, looking through the window in quest of outward objects, will show that your mind has not been abstracted, and will display to him at least your wish of not attending. He may, however, possibly have lost the habit of watching your eye for approbation; then you may assault his ear: if all other resources fail, beat with your foot that dead march of the spirits, that incessant tattoo, which so well deserves its name. Marvellous must be the patience of the much-enduring man whom some or other of these devices do not provoke: slight causes often produce great effects; the simple scratching of a pick-axe, properly applied to certain veins in a mine, will cause the most dreadful explosions.

Hitherto we have only professed to teach the defensive: let me now recommend to you the offensive part of the art of justification. As a supplement to reasoning comes recrimination: the pleasure of proving that you are right is surely incomplete till you have proved that your adversary is wrong; this might have been a secondary, let it now become a primary object with you; rest your own defence on it for further security: you are no longer to consider yourself as obliged either to deny, palliate, argue, or declaim, but simply to justify yourself by criminating another: all merit, you know, is judged of by comparison. In the art of recrimination, your memory will be of the highest service to you; for you are to open and keep an account-current of all the faults, mistakes, neglects, unkindnesses of those you live with; these you are to state against your own: I need not tell you that the balance will always be in your favour. In stating matters on opinion, produce the words of the very same person which passed days, months, years before, in contradiction to what he is then saying. By displacing, disjointing words and sentences, by misunderstanding the whole, or quoting only a part of what has been said, you may convict any man of inconsistency, particularly if he be a man of genius and feeling; for he speaks generally from the impulse of the moment, and of all others can the least bear to be charged with paradoxes. So far for a husband.

Recriminating is also of sovereign use in the quarrels of friends; no friend is so perfectly equable, so ardent in affection, so nice in punctilio, as never to offend: then "Note his faults, and con them all by rote."[75] Say you can forgive, but you can never forget; and surely it is much more generous to forgive and remember, than to forgive and forget. On every new alarm, call the unburied ghosts from former fields of battle; range them in tremendous array, call them one by one to witness against the conscience of your enemy, and ere the battle is begun take from him all courage to engage.

There is one case I must observe to you in which recrimination has peculiar poignancy. If you have had it in your power to confer obligations on any one, never cease reminding them of it: and let them feel that you have acquired an indefeasible right to reproach them without a possibility of their retorting. It is a maxim with some sentimental people, "To treat their servants as if they were their friends in distress." – I have observed that people of this cast make themselves amends, by treating their friends in distress as if they were their servants.

Apply this maxim – you may do it a thousand ways, especially in company. In general conversation, where every one is supposed to be on a footing, if any of your humble companions should presume to hazard an opinion contrary to yours, and should modestly begin with, "I think"; look as the man did when he said to his servant, "You think, sir – what business have you to think?"

Never fear to lose a friend by the habits which I recommend: reconciliations, as you have often heard it said – reconciliations are the cement of friendship; therefore friends should quarrel to strengthen their attachment, and offend each other for the pleasure of being reconciled.

I beg pardon for digressing: I was, I believe, talking of your husband, not of your friend – I have gone far out of the way.

If in your debates with your husband you should want "eloquence to vex him", the dull prolixity of narration, joined to the complaining monotony of voice which I formerly recommended, will supply its place, and have the desired effect: Somnus will prove propitious; then, ever and anon as the soporific charm begins to work, rouse him with interrogatories, such as, "Did not you say so? Don't you remember? Only answer me that!"

By-the-by, interrogatories artfully put may lead an unsuspicious reasoner, you know, always to your own conclusion.

In addition to the patience, philosophy, and other good things which Socrates learned from his wife, perhaps she taught him this mode of reasoning.

But, after all, the precepts of art, and even the natural susceptibility of your tempers, will avail you little in the sublime of our science, if you cannot command that ready enthusiasm which will make you enter into the part you are acting; that happy imagination which shall make you believe all you fear and all you invent.

Who is there amongst you who cannot or who will not justify when they are accused? Vulgar talent! the sublime of our science is to justify before we are accused. There is no reptile so vile but what will turn when it is trodden on; but of a nicer sense and nobler species are those whom nature has endowed with antennæ, which perceive and withdraw at the distant approach of danger. Allow me another allusion: similes cannot be crowded too close for a female taste; and analogy, I have heard, my fair pupils, is your favourite mode of reasoning.

The sensitive plant is too vulgar an allusion; but if the truth of modern naturalists may be depended upon, there is a plant which, instead of receding timidly from the intrusive touch, angrily protrudes its venomous juices upon all who presume to meddle with it: – do not you think this plant would be your fittest emblem?

Let me, however, recommend it to you, nice souls, who, of the mimosa kind, "fear the dark cloud, and feel the coming storm", to take the utmost precaution lest the same susceptibility which you cherish as the dear means to torment others should insensibly become a torment to yourselves.

Distinguish then between sensibility and susceptibility; between the anxious solicitude not to give offence, and the captious eagerness of vanity to prove that it ought not to have been taken; distinguish between the desire of praise and the horror of blame: can any two things be more different than the wish to improve, and the wish to demonstrate that you have never been to blame?

Observe, I only wish you to distinguish these things in your own minds; I would by no means advise you to discontinue the laudable practice of confounding them perpetually in speaking to others.

When you have nearly exhausted human patience in explaining, justifying, vindicating; when, in spite of all the pains you have taken, you have more than half betrayed your own vanity; you have a never-failing resource, in paying tribute to that of your opponent, as thus: –

"I am sure you must be sensible that I should never take so much pains to justify myself if I were indifferent to your opinion. – I know that I ought not to disturb myself with such trifles; but nothing is a trifle to me which concerns you. I confess I am too anxious to please; I know it's a fault, but I cannot cure myself of it now. – Too quick sensibility, I am conscious, is the defect of my disposition; it would be happier for me if I could be more indifferent, I know."

Who could be so brutal as to blame so amiable, so candid a creature? Who would not submit to be tormented with kindness?

When once your captive condescends to be flattered by such arguments as these, your power is fixed; your future triumphs can be bounded only by your own moderation; they are at once secured and justified.

Forbear not, then, happy pupils; but, arrived at the summit of power, give a full scope to your genius, nor trust to genius alone: to exercise in all its extent your privileged dominion, you must acquire, or rather you must pretend to have acquired, infallible skill in the noble art of physiognomy; immediately the thoughts as well as the words of your subjects are exposed to your inquisition.

Words may flatter you, but the countenance never can deceive you; the eyes are the windows of the soul, and through them you are to watch what passes in the inmost recesses of the heart. There, if you discern the slightest ideas of doubt, blame, or displeasure; if you discover the slightest symptoms of revolt, take the alarm instantly. Conquerors must maintain their conquests; and how easily can they do this, who hold a secret correspondence with the minds of the vanquished! Be your own spies then; from the looks, gestures, slightest motions of your enemies, you are to form an alphabet, a language intelligible only to yourselves, yet by which you shall condemn them; always remembering that in sound policy suspicion justifies punishment. In vain, when you accuse your friends of the high treason of blaming you, in vain let them plead their innocence, even of the intention. "They did not say a word which could be tortured into such a meaning." No, "but they looked daggers, though they used none."

And of this you are to be the sole judge, though there were fifty witnesses to the contrary.

How should indifferent spectators pretend to know the countenance of your friend as well as you do — you, that have a nearer, a dearer interest in attending to it? So accurate have been your observations, that no thought of their souls escapes you; nay, you often can tell even what they are going to think of.

The science of divination certainly claims your attention; beyond the past and the present, it shall extend your dominion over the future; from slight words, half-finished sentences, from silence itself, you shall draw your omens and auguries.

"I know what you were going to say"; or, "I know such a thing was a sign you were inclined to be displeased with me."

In the ardour of innocence, the culprit, to clear himself from such imputations, incurs the imputation of a greater offence. Suppose, to prove that you were mistaken, to prove that he could not have meant to blame you, he should declare that at the moment you mention, "You were quite foreign to his thoughts, he was not thinking at all about you."

Then in truth you have a right to be angry. To one of your class of justificators, this is the highest offence. Possessed as you are of the firm opinion that all persons, at all times, on all occasions, are intent upon you alone, is it not less mortifying to discover that you were thought ill of, than that you were not thought of at all? "Indifference, you know, sentimental pupils, is more fatal to love than even hatred."

Thus, my dear pupils, I have endeavoured to provide precepts adapted to the display of your several talents; but if there should be any amongst you who have no talents, who can neither argue nor persuade, who have neither sentiment nor enthusiasm, I must indeed – congratulate them; – they are peculiarly qualified for the science of Self-justification: indulgent nature, often even in the weakness, provides for the protection of her creatures; just Providence, as the guard of stupidity, has enveloped it with the impenetrable armour of obstinacy.

Fair idiots! let women of sense, wit, feeling, triumph in their various arts: yours are superior. Their empire, absolute as it sometimes may be, is perpetually subject to sudden revolutions. With them, a man has some chance of equal sway: with a fool he has none. Have they hearts and understandings? Then the one may be touched, or the other in some unlucky moment convinced; even in their very power lies their greatest danger: – not so with you. In vain let the most candid of his sex attempt to reason with you; let him begin with, "Now, my dear, only listen to reason": – you stop him at once with, "No, my dear, you know I do not pretend to reason; I only say, that's my opinion."

Let him go on to prove that yours is a mistaken opinion: – you are ready to acknowledge it long before he desires it. "You acknowledge it may be a wrong opinion; but still it is your opinion." You do not maintain it in the least, either because you believe it to be wrong or right, but merely because it is yours. Exposed as you might have been to the perpetual humiliation of being convinced, nature seems kindly to have denied you all perception of truth, or at least all sentiment of pleasure from the perception.

With an admirable humility, you are as well contented to be in the wrong as in the right; you answer all that can be said to you with a provoking humility of aspect.

"Yes; I do not doubt but what you say may be very true, but I cannot tell; I do not think myself capable of judging on these subjects; I am sure you must know much better than I do. I do not pretend to say but that your opinion is very just; but I own I am of a contrary way of thinking; I always thought so, and I always shall."

Should a man with persevering temper tell you that he is ready to adopt your sentiments if you will only explain them; should he beg only to have a reason for your opinion – no, you can give no reason. Let him urge you to say something in its defence: – no; like Queen Anne, you will only repeat the same thing over again, or be silent.[76] Silence is the ornament of your sex; and in silence, if there be not wisdom, there is safety. You will, then, if you please, according to your custom, sit listening to all entreaties to explain, and speak – with a fixed immutability of posture, and a pre-determined deafness of eye, which shall put your opponent utterly out of patience; yet still by persevering with the same complacent importance of countenance, you shall half persuade people you could speak if you would; you shall keep them in doubt by that true want of meaning, "which puzzles more than wit";[77] even because they cannot conceive the excess of your stupidity, they shall actually begin to believe that they themselves are stupid. Ignorance and doubt are the great parents of the sublime.

Your adversary, finding you impenetrable to argument, perhaps would try wit: – but, "On the impassive ice the lightnings play."[78] His eloquence or his kindness will avail less; when in yielding to you after a long harangue, he expects to please you, you will answer undoubtedly with the utmost propriety, "That you should be very sorry he yielded his judgment to you; that he is very good; that you are much obliged to him; but that, as to the point in dispute, it is a matter of perfect indifference to you; for your part, you have no choice at all about it; you beg that he will do just what he pleases; you know that it is the duty of a wife to submit; but you hope, however, you may have an *opinion* of your own."

Remember, all such speeches as these will lose above half their effect, if you cannot accompany them with the vacant stare, the insipid smile, the passive aspect of the humbly perverse.

Whilst I write, new precepts rush upon my recollection; but the subject is inexhaustible. I quit it with regret, though fully sensible of my presumption in having attempted to instruct those who, whilst they read, will smile in the consciousness of superior powers. Adieu! then, my fair readers: long may you prosper in the practice of an art peculiar to your sex! Long may you maintain unrivalled dominion at home and abroad; and long may your husbands rue the hour when first they made you promise "*to obey*"!

Written in 1787.
Published in 1795.

NOTES

Letter from a Gentleman to his Friend

1. Industrial workers such as handloomers were also considered susceptible to such deformities (See note 37 on "literary artisans").

2. This probably refers to Chaucer's fourteenth-century poem, "The Hous of Fame". In it, the goddess Fame allows access to her house as a reward and refuses admittance as punishment. Pope took up Chaucer's image in his *The Temple of Fame*. A short piece of Pope's, "To a Lady, *with the* Temple of Fame" (1715) adds an interesting gloss to eighteenth-century definitions of fame:

> What's Fame with Men, by Custom of the Nation,
> Is call'd in Women only Reputation

3. Edgeworth here is probably referring to "The Life of the Duke of Burgundy", contained in Madame La Fite's *Contes, Drames, et Entretiens*. The Edgeworths recommend this exemplary work in *Practical Education*. This particular observation, however, can be found in a poem by Thomas Newcomb, "An Epistle from the Duke of Burgundy to the French King" (1709). In it, the Duke reprimands his king for:

> Exchanging Camps for Beds of sinking Down

He warns the King:

> And while you thus, supine in lazy State,
> To Female guides commit your tottering throne

that

> Envied blessings Crown Brittania's Isle,
> By MARLBORO's Triumphs and in ANNA's Reign

We are left in no doubt that Queen Anne's triumphs are thanks to her commander and her son, just as her French rival's failures are the fault of his wife.

4. The gentleman is probably referring to some of the notorious women writers of the late seventeenth and early eighteenth century. Aphra Behn's (1640–89) plays were shocking enough, but her *Love Letters between a Nobleman and his Sister* (1683–7) caused outrage.

Lady Mary Wortley Montagu (1689–1762) and Delarivière Manley (1671–1724) both earned notoriety by satirizing "the secret histories of courts" in Montagu's *Court Poems* (1716) and Manley's *The Royal Mischief* (1696) and *The Court Legacy* (1733). Delarivière Manley's famous satire, *The New Atlantis* (1709) was considered particularly scandalous (See note 29).

5. This sentiment echoes arguments found in François de Salignac de la Mothe Fénelon, *Instructions for the Education of a Daughter* (1687, First English translation, 1707):

> What intrigues occur to us in history? what subversion of Laws and Manners? what bloody Wars? what Novelties in Religion? what Revolutions in State have been caused by the Irregularities of Women! Thus we have seen the necessity of a right Education of Daughters . . .

It is, however, worth noting that Fénelon produces these arguments *in favour* of female education.

6. Milton, *Paradise Lost* (1667), XI

> *Michael* from *Adam's* eyes the Filme remov'd
> Which that false fruit that promis'd clearer sight
> Had bred; then purg'd with Euphrasy and Rue
> The visual Nerve, for he had much to see

7. Prejudice is a key term in the eighteenth-century debates about the possibility of objective knowledge. Mrs Barbauld's essay "On Prejudice" warns that communication is always impeded by cultural conditioning, or our "horizons", as she puts it. Dugald Stewart treads a cautious middle ground, stressing the need for the philosopher to "unlearn the errors to which he had been taught to give an implicit assent, before the dawn of reason and reflection", but also warning against "the dangers of unlimited scepticism".

8. William Coxe (1747–1828) was a teacher and historian. As tutor to the son of the Earl of Pembroke, he travelled through Switzerland and Russia. He published his travels in several volumes. Edgeworth probably drew this anecdote from *Travels into Poland, Russia, Sweden, and Denmark*, 3 vols (1784).

9. In *The Rape of the Lock* (1712), Alexander Pope (1688–1744) rouses the mortified Belinda to righteous anger against her assaulter by having Spleen visit her. This "wayward queen" is the "parent of vapours and of female wit" (IV).

10. Catherine de' Medici (1519–89) was born in Florence into the famous Renaissance family. In order to forge an alliance between Rome and France, her uncle arranged her marriage with Henry, Duke of Orléans, the second son of Francis I. The early and unexpected deaths of her brother and father-in-law led to her becoming Queen of France in 1547. By 1559 she was a widow; but in the face of resentment and

suspicion she ruled for her young son, Francis, and went on to govern after his death. Her reign was marked by bitter intrigue and wars.

11. Original note: Dugald Stewart

Dugald Stewart (1753–1828) was Professor of Moral Philosophy at Edinburgh University, and was closely involved in a group of Scottish empiricists which included David Hume, Adam Ferguson and Adam Smith. Maria Edgeworth and her father met him when they visited Edinburgh in 1803. Afterwards, Edgeworth kept up a correspondence with Stewart's wife, and stayed with them when she visited Scotland again, in 1823.

12. Just such a complaint is found in a contemporary essay by a woman educated well above the standards of the day. In "On the Insensibility of the Men to the Charms of a Female Mind Cultivated with Polite and Solid Literature. In a Letter" (1779), Vicesimus Knox explains how her father taught her the classics and history, as well as music and dancing. She complains that:

> My own sex stands too much in awe of me to bear me any affection . . . I am avoided by gentlemen who are ambitious of the company of other ladies. They have dropt, in the hearing of some of my friends, that though they find me extremely clever, yet they cannot reconcile the ideas of female attractions and the knowledge of the Greek.

13. Isaac D'Israeli's *Curiosities of Literature* gathered together historical surveys and anecdotes, and organized them under various headings. The section on "A Literary Wife" offers a brief history of the wives of literary men, and discusses the relative merits of education and ignorance.

14. Madame Anne Dacier (1654–1720) edited and translated classical texts into French. In "A Literary Wife" (see above) D'Israeli offers the following opinion:

> It was peculiar to the learned Dacier to be united to a woman, his equal in erudition and his superior in taste.

Other British writers also mention her as a prototype of the female scholar. Mary Astell, for example, cautions her readers:

> Let therefore the famous Madam *D'acier* . . . excite the Emulation of the English Ladies.
> (A Serious Proposal to the Ladies, for the Advancement of their True and Greatest Interest, 1694)

15. Jean le Rond d'Alembert (1717–83) was a philosopher and mathematician of the French Enlightenment. He is best remembered as co-editor, with Diderot, of the *Encyclopédie: ou Dictionnaire raisonné des sciences, des arts, et des métiers* (1751–80). His contributions to this monument to rational knowledge included its "Discours Préliminaire",

and several polemical articles. In *Ormond* (1817), Edgeworth has her worthy hero, Harry Ormond, meet d'Alembert in Paris. We hear he is "simple, open-hearted, unpresuming, and cheerful in society".

16. Apicius was a celebrated Roman gourmet. A cookery book bearing his name appeared some centuries after his death.

17. This phrase originally occurs in Shakespeare's *Hamlet*. Early in the play, Horatio and Hamlet discuss Hamlet's father, the dead king of Denmark. Hamlet mournfully remarks:

> A was a man, take him for all in all,
> I shall not look upon his like again
> (I, ii)

18. Hercules-Spinster was probably an eighteenth-century strong-man.

19. Mount Parnassus is sacred to Dionysus, Apollo, and the Muses. It represents the world of poetry.

20. Molière (1622–73) is the author of many famous French comedies, including *Les Femmes Savantes*. First performed in 1722, it was generally received as an attack on female pedantry. It is set in the household of the "bon bourgeois" Chrysale and his wife Philaminte. Philaminte thinks only of literature and science, and neglects her domestic duties. She goes so far as to fire her maid, Martine, because she is a "friponne" who does not speak according to the rigid grammatical rules of Vaugelas. Philaminte's husband weakly protests:

> Je vis de bonne soupe et non de beau langage
> Vaugelas n'apprend point à bien faire un potage (II, vii)

> (I desire good soups not fine language; Vaugelas has no idea how to make good soup.)

21. At the start of the play, Othello is called upon to explain how Desdemona fell in love with him. Her father, the senator, Brabantio, accuses him of using spells and medicines. Othello replies:

> I will a round unvarnish'd tale deliver
> Of my whole course of love
> (I, iii)

(This phrase recurs in the Preface to *Castle Rackrent*.) Othello recounts how, at the request of the senator, he told the story of his life:

> Wherein I spake of most disastrous chances,
> Of moving accidents by flood and field;
> Of hairbreadth scapes i' th' imminent deadly breach
> . . .
> It was my hint to speak such – was the process:
> And of the Cannibals that each other eat,
> The Anthropophagi, and men whose heads

Do grow beneath their shoulders. This to hear
Would Desdemona seriously incline;
But still the house arrairs would draw her thence;
Which ever as she could with haste dispatch,
She'd come again, and with a greedy ear
Devour up my discourse.
(I, iii)

22. Catalepsy is a disease characterized by a seizure or long-lasting trance. In the late eighteenth century it was associated with nervous disorders.

23. This may be Sir John Harrington (d.1582), who wrote two poems laying out the duties of a wife, "Husband to Wife" and "Wife to Husband". Both were written in 1564 and published in 1775.

Answer to the Preceding Letter

24. This is possibly another reference to *The Rape of the Lock*, where, in the battle scene, "Men, monkeys, lapdogs, parrots, perish all" (IV).

25. Sir William Hamilton (1730–1803) was a diplomat and archaeologist. In 1764 he was appointed British envoy extraordinary to the court of Naples. As well as performing crucial diplomatic duties he took a keen interest in volcanic phenomena. Hamilton ascended Mount Vesuvius no less than twenty-two times, and actually witnessed it erupt in 1776 and 1777. His "Observations on Mount Vesuvius" were published amongst his *Philosophical Transactions* (1766–80). Hamilton sold several significant collections to the British Museum, not just of volcanic earth and minerals, but also of Greek vases. Josiah Wedgwood, a member of the same Lunar circle as Richard Lovell Edgeworth, claimed that Hamilton bringing this collection to Britain made his own pottery designs possible. Sir William Hamilton is, however, more widely remembered as the husband of "Emma Hart", or Amy Lyon, who became Nelson's mistress.

26. Necromancy is the practice of conjuring up the dead, in order to obtain knowledge of the future. It is sometimes mentioned in late eighteenth-century Gothic novels.

27. This is a point made by Dugald Stewart in his *Elements of the Philosophy of the Human Mind* vol. I (1792). (See note 11):

> It is too, in times of general darkness and barbarism, that what is commonly called originality of genius most frequently appears: and surely the great aim of an enlightened philosophy, is not to rear a small number of individuals, who may be regarded as prodigies in an ignorant and admiring age, but to diffuse, as widely as possible, that degree of cultivation which may enable the bulk of a people to possess all the intellectual and moral improvement of which their nature is susceptible.

28. "The poor woman," they exclaimed, "has only one leg."

29. Jonathan Swift (1667–1745) was Dean of St Patrick's Cathedral in Dublin. Much of his poetry and prose casts a decidedly satiric eye upon English and Irish public life. "Stella" was Swift's mistress, Esther Johnson (1681–1728), whom he had persuaded to move to Dublin in 1701. The *Journal to Stella*, written between 1710 and 1713, consisted of letters written by Swift from London. In them he either complains of Stella's tardy responses to his letters, or details the faults he finds in the letters he does receive. Swift combines expressions of tender concern for her health (she had very poor eyesight) with cruel barbs on her epistolary style:

> *R*ediculous, madam? I supose you mean ridiculous: let me have no more of that; it is the author of *Atlantis*'s spelling. I have mended it in your letter.
> (Letter the Eleventh)

Edgeworth is here referring to the feigned surprise of a later letter:

> Pray Stella, explain those two words of yours to me, what do you mean by *villian and dainger*?
> (Letter the Nineteenth)

30. References to Turkey in particular and the Orient in general were very much in vogue in late eighteenth-century literature and letters. Lady Mary Wortley Montagu's "Embassy Letters" and "Turkish Letters" were published in her *Letters* (1765–7).

31. Erasmus Darwin (1731–1802) made this famous claim in the Advertisement to "The Loves of the Plants", Part II of *The Botanic Garden* (1791). This long poem set out to explain "the sexual system of Linneus", a Swedish naturalist. The Advertisement announces:

> The general design of the following sheets is to enlist Imagination under the banners of Science, and to lead her votaries from the looser analogies, which dress out the image of poetry, to the stricter ones, which form the ratiocination of philosophy.

Darwin was a friend of Richard Lovell Edgeworth, and also an influential member of the Birmingham Lunar Circle. Both Maria Edgeworth and her father admired his happy combinations of poetry, science and philosophy. Charles Darwin (1809–82) was his grandson.

32. This proverb was sometimes quoted in the eighteenth century as the basic rationale for conservative economics.

33. This phrase is from *Hesiod: or, the Rise of Woman* (1722) by Thomas Parnell (1679–1718). It recounts the story of women's development:

Young *Hermes* next, a close-contriving God,
Her Brows encircled with his Serpent Rod:
Then Plots and Fair Excuses, fill's her Brain,
The Views of breaking am'rous Vows for Gain,
The Price of favours; the designing Arts
That aim at Richer in Contempt of Hearts;
And for a Comfort in the Marriage Life,
The little, pilf'ring Temper of a *Wife*

34. Original note: Stedman's Voyage to Surinam, Vol. II, p. 47.
John Gabriel Stedman, *Narrative of a Five Year's Expedition against the Revolted Negroes of Surinam, on the wild coast of South America, from the year 1772 to 1777* (1796), Vol. II. Stedman (1714–97) was born in Holland of an English father and a Dutch mother. He joined the army and in 1772 he volunteered to join an expedition sent by the States General to quell a revolt in Surinam (Dutch Guiana). His account of the journey and his time in Surinam shocked contemporary European opinion, not only because of its declared sympathy with the rebels, but also because in it he describes his relationship with a native woman.

35. One of the examples uppermost in the late eighteenth-century mind would have been Mary Wollstonecraft (1759–97). Her support of the French Revolution against Edmund Burke's criticisms offended conservative political opinion, and her claims for women's rights were similarly shocking. It was, however, Wollstonecraft's own sexual morality which caused the most outrage. Mary Hays (1760–1843), author of the radical novel *Memoirs of Emma Courtney* (1796) was also criticized for both her public writings and private actions. Amelia Opie's novel *Adeline Mowbray: Mother and Daughter* (1804) makes this link between loose thoughts and loose morals clear. In it, the heroine's political idealism leads her into tragic ruin.

Edgeworth admired Fanny Burney (1752–1840) and Anna Laetitia Barbauld (1743–1825), and probably has them in mind as positive examples of female authorship. Fanny Burney's education was supervised by her father, much as Edgeworth's own was; and all Mrs Barbauld's work is marked by a strong commitment to education.

36. Many of the debates of the early Christian Church are marked by just such a concern for minute detail.

37. Original note: Professor Dugald Stewart, *History of the Philosophy of the Human Mind*.
In *Elements of the Philosophy of the Human Mind* (see note 27), Dugald Stewart discusses professions in which:

A man of very confined acquisitions may arrive at first eminence; and in which he will perhaps be the more likely to excel, the more he has concentrated the whole force of his mind to one particular object. But such a person, however distinguished in his own sphere, is merely to be a literary artisan; and neither attains the perfection, or the happiness, of his nature. "That education can only be considered as complete and generous, which, (in the language of Milton) fits a man to perform justly, skilfully, and magnanimously, all the offices, both private and public, of peace and of war.

Underlying all of this is a firm Enlightenment belief that it is every man's duty not to seek eminence but:

> to render himself happy as an individual, and an agreeable, a respectable, and a useful member of society.

38. In *Practical Education* (1798), the Edgeworths cite this example in another context:

> Sometimes a question that appears simple involves the consideration of others that are difficult . . . For instance, if a child was to hear that the Dutch burn and destroy quantities of spice, the produce of their Indian islands, he would probably express some surprise, and perhaps some indignation . . . (p. 686)

39. In the *Iliad*, Ajax the son of Telamon, competes with Odysseus (in Latin, Ulysses) for the armour of Achilles. Homer characterizes Ajax as brave but slow-witted whereas Odysseus is victorious because he is clever and enterprising.

40. This refers to the legend of King Arthur.

41. Original note: Condorcet, *History of the Progress of the Human Mind*.

Marie Jean Antoine Nicolas Caritat, Marquis de Condorcet (1743–94) was the only member of the French Encyclopédistes to participate in the French Revolution. In 1793 he strongly defended the Girondin constitution against the Jacobin one, and was forced into hiding. While living in seclusion in Paris, he worked on his *Sketch for a Historical Picture of the Progress of the Human Mind*, which was published posthumously in 1795.

42. This term echoes contemporary debate about women's legislative as well as educational rights. Mary Wollstonecraft's *A Vindication of the Rights of Woman* (1792) revises her earlier *A Vindication of the Rights of Men* (1790), which challenged Edmund Burke's conservative horror of the French Revolution. The terms of the debate are thus already revolutionary; and in 1795 fatally associated with fears of France and 1789. Yet curiously enough, the term features in the 1798 Advertisement to the second edition of *Letters for Literary Ladies*, when Edgeworth stresses the importance of "asserting more strongly the female right to literature".

43. As archon of Athens, Themistocles was responsible for creating and commanding the Athenian navy in the fifth century. He laid the basis of Athen's later trading supremacy.

44. This story is found in Samuel Johnson, *The History of Rasselas, Prince of Abyssinia*, 2 vols (1759). After much travelling, the prince, Rasselas, decides to devote his life to learning. His companion, Imlac, warns him of the hazards of such a life, by recounting the anxieties of a learned astronomer:

> I have possessed for five years the regulation of the weather, and the distribution of the seasons: the sun has listened to my dictates, and passed from tropick to tropick at my direction; the clouds at my call, have poured their waters, and the Nile has overflowed at my command . . . The winds alone, of all the elemental powers, have hitherto refused my authority, and multitudes have perished by equinoctial tempests which I have found myself unable to prohibit or restrain. I have administered this great office with exact justice, and made to the different nations of the earth an impartial dividend of rain and sunshine. What must have been the misery of half the globe, if I had limited the clouds to particular regions, or confined the sun to either side of the equator?

All this is to teach the Prince the dangers of allowing the imagination to dominate over reason.

45. Lord Kenyon (1732–1802) was a judge who was made Master of the Rolls in 1784. He was known for his public stance on issues of morality.

46. In *Emile, ou De l'Education* (1762), Jean Jacques Rousseau (1712–78) bases his theories of female education on his belief that

> Woman is a coquette by profession, but her coquetry varies with her aims; let these aims be in accordance with those of nature, and a woman will receive a fitting education.

He praises "genuine coquetry", "honest coquetry", and "the coquetry of true love". Women are sirens because, as Edgeworth realizes, Rousseau's praise of coquetry slides into a condemnation of women. For, despite Rousseau's praise, coquetry is a "dangerous weapon" which will distract men from "the discussion of pure reason".

47. Original note: Vide Plutarch

Plutarch's *Lives of Caesar, Brutus, and Antony* portrays Antony and Cleopatra's love as a "sweet poison". This is thought to be the principal source of Shakespeare's *Antony and Cleopatra*, although many versions of the story exist.

48. In *Emile*, Rousseau also declares that:

> Cunning is the natural gift of women, and so convinced am I that all our natural inclinations are right, that I would cultivate this among others, only guarding against its abuse.

Fluency of address also comes naturally to women:

Women have ready tongues; they talk earlier, more easily, and more pleasantly than men. They are also said to talk more; this may be true, but I am prepared to reckon it to their credit; eyes and mouth are equally busy for the same cause.

On dissimulation, we have to follow Edgeworth into a footnote, where Rousseau complains that:

The kind of deceit referred to here is just the opposite of that deceit becoming in a woman, and taught her by nature . . .

49. Original note: See the introduction of Cupid to the Muses and Minerva, in a charming poem of Mrs Barbauld's, "The origin of song writing". Would it not afford a beautiful subject for a picture?

In the poem, Venus introduces the wayward child Cupid to the Muses. He is "artless yet and young" and she beseeches them to "refine his air, and smooth his tongue". Edgeworth is referring to the unexpected outcome of this meeting, which is to make love the proper subject of poetry:

Now of power his darts are found,
Twice ten thousand times to wound.
Now no more the slackened strings
Breathe of high immortal things,
But Cupid tunes the Muse's lyre
To languid notes of soft desire.
In every clime, in every tongue,
'Tis love inspires the poet's song.

50. Original note: Milton

This refers to a description of beauty in Milton's mask, *Comus* (1637):

Beauty is natures brag, and must be shown
In courts, at feasts, and high solemnities
Where most may wonder at the workmanship;
It is for homely features to keep home,
They had their name thence; coarse complexions
And cheeks of sorry grain will serve to ply

51. Original note: Appendix to *Monthly Review*, from January to April 1798, p. 516.

52. This probably refers to William Robertson (1721–93) whose writings included histories of America and of India. Dugald Stewart wrote the preface to his *Works* in 1817.

53. A look of excitement, wit, nobility and propriety. The spirit of French women was seen in the "pretty little face denoting wit and coquetry".

54. In *The Fable of the Bees* (1714–25) Bernard Mandeville (1670?–1733) argues that private vices are public benefits. Edgeworth here introduces the domestic woman into the allegory, and thus shifts the emphasis from vice to virtue.

55. Original note: J. Anderson, *Essay on the Management of a Dairy.*

James Anderson (1739–1808) was a Scottish farmer who published extensively on agriculture and economics. His demands for protection for Scottish fisheries led to a long correspondence with Jeremy Bentham. Anderson's first wife died in 1788.

56. According to Johnson's *Lives of the Poets* (1779–81), Lyttleton "married Miss Lucy Fortescue of Devonshire ... with whom he appears to have lived in the highest degree of connubial felicity: but human pleasures are short; she died in childbed about five years afterwards, and he solaced his grief by writing a long poem to her memory." This is the "Monody to his Wife" from which Edgeworth quotes on the title page of *Belinda* (1801).

D'Israeli's "A Literary Wife" records that Baron Haller "inspired his wife and family with a taste for different pursuits" (See note 13).

Letters of Julia and Caroline

57. Addison, *Cato: a Tragedy* (1713), III, v.

58. William Shakespeare, *Richard III* (See note 63).

59. Original note: Hume said, that Parnell's poems were as fresh at the twentieth reading as at the first.

60. In Shakespeare's *King John*, Lewis, the Dauphin bitterly complains:

There's nothing in this world can make me joy.
Life is as tedious as a twice-told tale
Vexing the dull ear of a drowsy man;
And bitter shame hath spoil'd the sweet world's taste,
That it yields nought but shame and bitterness.
(III, iv)

61. Edmund Waller (1605–87) published a "Panegyric" on the death of Oliver Cromwell, which Samuel Johnson describes as "dictated by real veneration for his memory". Waller's contemporaries were less than impressed when he swiftly followed this with his "Congratulation" welcoming the Restoration of Charles II. In his *Lives of the Poets*, Vol. I, Johnson recounts the following anecdote:

The "Congratulation" was considered inferior in poetical merit to the "Panegyric"; and it is reported that when the king told Waller of the disparity, he answered, "Poets, Sir, succeed better in fiction than in truth".

62. "Animal magnetism" is the eighteenth-century scientific term for what was more popularly known as mesmerism. In 1779 Frantz Anton Mesmer (1734–1815) published his *Mémoire sur la découverte du magnétisme animal*, and its influence spread throughout Europe. Its exponents held that the body was filled with fluids which could be manipulated between magnetic poles. Faith in the medical effects of such work may have been on the wane, as Edgeworth claims; but a generation of Romantic poets were discovering the artistic possibilities of animal magnetism. Coleridge, Shelley, and Browning all glimpsed in mesmerism the operations of the imagination, and the source of poetry.

63. These lines are spoken by the despairing Richard III at the end of Shakespeare's *Richard III*. The second part of the speech is now more famous:

Slave, I have set my life upon a cast
And I will stand the hazard of the die
I think there be six Richmonds in the field;
Five I have slain to-day instead of him.
A horse! a horse! my kingdom for a horse!
(V, iv)

64. This phrase echoes Othello's reaction when Iago accuses Desdemona of adultery: "Farewell! Othello's occupation gone" (III, iii).

65. In Shakespeare's *Macbeth*, a bloody child appears to Macbeth and tells him that, "none of woman born shall harm Macbeth" (IV, i). Edgeworth is quoting from his response:

Then live, Macduff; what need I fear of thee?
But yet I'll make assurance double sure
And take a bond of fate.
(IV, i)

66. Gaius Mæcenas (c.70–8 BC) was a Roman diplomat in the court of Augustus. He wrote some poetry himself, and his wealth and prestige made it possible for him to become a powerful patron of the arts. Virgil and Horace were among those whom he favoured.

67. Francis Bacon's (1561–1620) philosophy was committed to the exploration and acquisition of knowledge. In the eighteenth century his theory of progress via scientific advances was widely admired by French Enlightenment philosophers, and the Scottish empiricists also praised his arguments on learning. In his own lifetime, however, Bacon's philosophic reputation was compromised by his role as courtier, and this is probably the scandal to which Julia refers. He was appointed Lord Chancellor in 1618, but by 1621 he had admitted to charges of bribery. He was disqualified from Parliament, excluded from Court, and briefly imprisoned. That ended his public career.

An Essay on the Noble Science of Self-Justification

68. This is another quotation from *Hesiod: or, the Rise of Woman* by Thomas Parnell. This stages an earlier moment in woman's history:

> Gold scepter'd Juno next exalts the Fair;
> Her touch endows her with imperious Air,
> Self-valuing Fancy, highly-crested Pride,
> Strong sov'reign Will, and some Desire to chide:
> For which, an Eloquence, that aims to vex,
> With native Tropes of Anger, arms the sex.

69. In the Christian Church, the doctrine of infallibility refers to the inability to err in the teaching of revealed truths. The seat of infallibility was a vexed issue in the early Church, but receded into the background until the Roman Catholic Church revived papal infallibility in 1870.

70. In philosophy, this refers to the resolution of dense moral dilemmas. It is more commonly associated with specious or misleading reasoning. In the latter context, in the eighteenth century it was often associated with the rigorous intellectual tradition of Roman Catholic Jesuit priests.

71. Somnus is the Roman god of sleep.

72. Original note: Marmontel.

Marmontel (1723–99) was the author of *Les Contes Moraux*, tales much admired by the Edgeworths. When Harry Ormond, hero of *Ormond* (1817) (See note 15) has his first glimpse of salon society in Paris, he encounters a reformed Marmontel, who preaches the virtues of a domestic life. The narrative breaks into a rare moment of enthusiasm:

> Marmontel was distinguished for combining in his conversation, as in his character, two quantities for which there are no precise English words, *naïveté* and *finesse*. Whoever is acquainted with Marmontel's writings must have a perfect knowledge of what is meant by both.

73. Original note: Emilius and Sophia.

In *Emile*, Rousseau employs what is here called "paradoxical language" to make his point. His style is part of his argument, in so far as it allows him to twist the discourse of reason to his theoretical advantage.

74. Original note: Hume.

David Hume (1711–76) was a Scottish empiricist whose philosophies had an enormous influence on late eighteenth-century literature. His works include *A Treatise on Human Nature* (1739–40), and several volumes of *Essays* and *Inquiries*.

75. This echoes a speech in Shakespeare's *Julius Caesar*. Cassius and Brutus, two of the conspirators against Julius Caesar, are arguing. After listening to Brutus's charges against him, Cassius replies:

> For Cassius is aweary of the world:
> Hated by one he loves; brav'd by his brother;
> Check'd like a bondman; all his faults observ'd,
> Set in a notebook, learn'd, and conn'd by rote,
> To cast in my teeth.
> (IV, iii)

76. Original note: Duchess of Marlborough's Apology.
Sarah Churchill, Duchess of Marlborough was Mistress of the Robes to Queen Anne. They had a stormy relationship, which culminated in the publication of *An Account of the Conduct of the Dowager Duchess of Marlborough* (1742).

77. In Alexander Pope's notorious *Of the Characters of Woman: an Epistle to a Lady* (1734–5), the poet bitterly complains:

> Woman and Fool are two hard things to hit
> For true No-meaning puzzles more than Wit

78. Pope, *Temple of Fame* (See note 2).

SUGGESTIONS FOR FURTHER READING

Unfortunately, there are no published essays or articles which deal specifically with *Letters for Literary Ladies*. It is, however, discussed in Marilyn Butler's excellent biography of Edgeworth, *Maria Edgeworth: A Literary Biography* (Oxford, 1972). Butler's research is invaluable for any account of Edgeworth's writings.

Recent work on Edgeworth has tended to re-read her texts within the structures of colonialism. Tom Dunne's *Maria Edgeworth and the Colonial Mind* (Dublin, 1985) was one of the first such essays. His "'A gentleman's estate should be a moral school': Edgeworthstown in fact and fiction", in Gillespie and Moran eds, *Longford: Essays in County History* (Dublin, 1990) also clarifies her specific political agenda. W. J. McCormack's *Ascendancy and Tradition in Anglo–Irish Literary History, 1789–1939* (Oxford, 1989) discusses Edgeworth's Irish novels in the context of the invention of an Anglo–Irish tradition.

Although slightly older, Michael Hurst's *Maria Edgeworth and the Public Scene* (London, 1969) is also useful in terms of the wider public context of Edgeworth's work. Older still is Helen Zimmern's *Maria Edgeworth* (London, 1883) – which belongs to a series called "Men of Letters"! It gives a marvellous insight into Victorian opinions on Edgeworth and her father, and also shows how the meanings of her life and works have shifted over time.

More generally, some of the recent work on women and education in the eighteenth century is very useful. Elizabeth Kowaleski-Wallace's "Milton's Daughters: The Education of Eighteenth-Century Women Writers", *Feminist Studies* (12) 2, Summer 1986, pp. 275–89 deals specifically with Edgeworth and Hannah More. Alice Browne, *The Eighteenth-Century Feminist Mind* (Brighton, 1988) and K. M. Rogers, *Feminism in Eighteenth-Century England* (Brighton, 1982) put Edgeworth in the context of her peers. Vivien Jones's anthology of eighteenth-century texts, *Women in the Eighteenth Century: Constructions of Femininity* (London and New York, 1990), is perhaps the best place to begin re-reading Edgeworth, as it makes visible the systems of national, sexual, and generic difference which define *Letters for Literary Ladies*.

TEXT SUMMARY

Letter from a Gentleman to His Friend, upon the Birth of a Daughter, pp.1–14

The gentleman advises his friend to consider carefully his determination to educate his daughter, for it can only bring unhappiness to all concerned. A woman cannot benefit from education because she has neither the aptitude nor the time for it and, given her role in society as a paragon of honour and virtue, no need for it, either. Moreover, such "educated" women as do exist invariably lack modesty and discretion; are treated with envy rather than friendship and are unlikely to find a husband because a man does not want a wife whose talents match his own.

Answer to the Preceding Letter, pp.15–38

The friend replies to – and disagrees with – nearly every point the gentleman has raised. A woman has just as much ability to learn, but she has not been given the opportunity. Since she does not have to work to support her family, she has plenty of free time to gain greater understanding. Honour and virtue are all the more worthy when they stem from instincts which, while instilled at childhood, have been carefully reflected upon. And, as a woman's understanding increases, she will learn modesty and discretion and will be regarded as a worthy friend and wife.

Letters of Julia and Caroline

Letter I, Julia to Caroline, pp.39–41

Julia tells her contemplative friend that it is useless to urge her to reflect rather than simply to feel. She has no wish to replace her passionate sensibilities with a philosopher's tranquillity. Besides, a woman should not philosophize; her role in life is solely to please and she is prized the more highly for being weak.

Letter II, Caroline's Answer to Julia, pp.42–46

Caroline asks Julia why she wishes so much to please and proposes that her desire stems from the stronger desire of wanting praise. Caroline admits to the same desire, but she is more discriminating as to the praise's source and urges Julia to be equally discerning, for the sake of her future happiness.

Letter III, Caroline to Julia on her intended marriage, pp.46–50

Caroline tries to give impartial advice to Julia, who is trying to decide whether to marry Lord V— or Caroline's brother. If she married the former, Caroline predicts, she would have wealth and status but could not expect companionship from her husband. And her time would be so taken up with society life that she would lose all opportunity for many activities she currently enjoys. If, however, she married the latter, she would enjoy a lifelong friendship with someone who shared many similar interests, although she would not have such elevated social standing.

Letter IV, Caroline to Lady V— Upon her intended separation from her husband, pp.50–55

Julia is in despair. She wishes she had not married Lord V—. All Caroline's predictions have come true. Caroline, however, tries to dissuade her friend from leaving her husband, pointing out that if she did, she would almost certainly be outcast by society. It would be far better if she devoted her time to her family, thereby earning society's respect and, as a result, her husband's affection.

Letter V, Caroline to Lady V— On her conduct after her separation from her husband, pp.55–57

In abrupt tones, Caroline expresses dismay at Julia's reckless behaviour, which is causing great concern amongst her family and friends. She begs Julia to reconsider what she has done, to accept a friend's assistance, and to return to her family.

Letter VI, Caroline to Lady V— Just before she went to France, pp.57–58

Seeing that she has no influence at all over Julia's behaviour, Caroline laments that she must end their friendship. She foresees nothing but unhappiness for her childhood friend, but sees, too, that there is nothing she can do to prevent it.

Letter VII, Caroline to Lord V— Written a few months after the date of the preceding letter, pp.58–62

With some temerity, Caroline writes to Julia's husband. She has received a letter from Julia, who is in great distress. Tracing her to an inn, she brings her home to recover from illness brought on by remorse at her ill conduct. But Caroline's help comes too late.

An Essay on the Noble Science of Self-Justification, pp.63–77

Opening with the premise that a lady can do no wrong, the author sets out to prove that no matter her position or intelligence, a woman can always win any argument, no matter how superior her adversary.

CLASSIC FICTION
IN EVERYMAN

A SELECTION

Frankenstein
MARY SHELLEY
A masterpiece of Gothic terror in its original 1818 version **£3.99**

Dracula
BRAM STOKER
One of the best known horror stories in the world **£3.99**

The Diary of A Nobody
GEORGE AND WEEDON GROSSMITH
A hilarious account of suburban life in Edwardian London **£4.99**

Some Experiences and Further Experiences of an Irish R. M.
SOMERVILLE AND ROSS
Gems of comic exuberance and improvisation **£4.50**

Three Men in a Boat
JEROME K. JEROME
English humour at its best **£2.99**

Twenty Thousand Leagues under the Sea
JULES VERNE
Scientific fact combines with fantasy in this prophetic tale of underwater adventure **£4.99**

The Best of Father Brown
G. K. CHESTERTON
An irresistible selection of crime stories – unique to Everyman **£3.99**

The Collected Raffles
E. W. HORNUNG
Dashing exploits from the most glamorous figure in crime fiction **£4.99**

£2.99

£5.99

£5.99

CLASSIC NOVELS
IN EVERYMAN

A SELECTION

The Way of All Flesh
SAMUEL BUTLER
A savagely funny odyssey from joy-
less duty to unbridled liberalism **£4.99**

Born in Exile
GEORGE GISSING
A rationalist's progress towards love
and compromise in class-ridden
Victorian England **£4.99**

David Copperfield
CHARLES DICKENS
One of Dickens' best-loved novels,
brimming with humour **£3.99**

The Last Chronicle of Barset
ANTHONY TROLLOPE
Trollope's magnificent conclusion
to his Barsetshire novels **£4.99**

He Knew He Was Right
ANTHONY TROLLOPE
Sexual jealousy, money and
women's rights within marriage –
a novel ahead of its time **£6.99**

Tess of the D'Urbervilles
THOMAS HARDY
The powerful, poetic classic of
wronged innocence **£3.99**

Wuthering Heights
and Poems
EMILY BRONTE
A powerful work of genius – one of
the great masterpieces of literature
£3.50

Tom Jones
HENRY FIELDING
The wayward adventures of one of
literatures most likable heroes **£5.99**

The Master of Ballantrae
and Weir of Hermiston
R. L. STEVENSON
Together in one volume, two great
novels of high adventure and family
conflict **£4.99**

£3.99

£2.99

£3.99

AVAILABILITY
All books are available from your local bookshop or direct from
**Littlehampton Book Services Cash Sales, 14 Eldon Way, LinesideEstate,
Littlehampton, West Sussex BN17 7HE.** PRICES ARE SUBJECT TO CHANGE.

To order any of the books, please enclose a cheque (in £ sterling) made payable to
Littlehampton Book Services, or phone your order through with credit card details (Access,
Visa or Mastercard) on 0903 721596 (24 hour answering service) stating card number and
expiry date. Please add £1.25 for package and postage to the total value of your order.

ESSAYS, CRITICISM AND HISTORY IN EVERYMAN

A SELECTION

The Embassy to Constantinople and Other Writings

LIUDPRAND OF CREMONA
An insider's view of political machinations in medieval Europe **£5.99**

The Rights of Man

THOMAS PAINE
One of the great masterpieces of English radicalism **£4.99**

Speeches and Letters

ABRAHAM LINCOLN
A key document of the American Civil War **£4.99**

Essays

FRANCIS BACON
An excellent introduction to Bacon's incisive wit and moral outlook **£3.99**

Puritanism and Liberty: Being the Army Debates (1647-49) from the Clarke Manuscripts

A fascinating revelation of Puritan minds in action **£7.99**

History of His Own Time

BISHOP GILBERT BURNET
A highly readable contemporary account of the Glorious Revolution of 1688 **£7.99**

Biographia Literaria

SAMUEL TAYLOR COLERIDGE
A masterpiece of criticism, marrying the study of literature with philosophy **£4.99**

Essays on Literature and Art

WALTER PATER
Insights on culture and literature from a major voice of the 1890s **£3.99**

Chesterton on Dickens: Criticisms and Appreciations

A landmark in Dickens criticism, rarely surpassed **£4.99**

Essays and Poems

R. L. STEVENSON
Stevenson's hidden treasures in a new selection **£4.99**

£3.99

£4.99

WOMEN'S WRITING
IN EVERYMAN

A SELECTION

Female Playwrights of the Restoration
FIVE COMEDIES
Rediscovered literary treasures in a unique selection **£5.99**

The Secret Self
SHORT STORIES BY WOMEN
'A superb collection' *Guardian* **£4.99**

Short Stories
KATHERINE MANSFIELD
An excellent selection displaying the remarkable range of Mansfield's talent **£3.99**

Women Romantic Poets 1780-1830: An Anthology
Hidden talent from the Romantic era, rediscovered for the first time **£5.99**

Selected Poems
ELIZABETH BARRETT BROWNING
A major contribution to our appreciation of this inspiring and innovative poet **£5.99**

Frankenstein
MARY SHELLEY
A masterpiece of Gothic terror in its original 1818 version **£3.99**

The Life of Charlotte Brontë
MRS GASKELL
A moving and perceptive tribute by one writer to another **£4.99**

Vindication of the Rights of Woman and The Subjection of Women
MARY WOLLSTONECRAFT
AND J. S. MILL
Two pioneering works of early feminist thought **£4.99**

The Pastor's Wife
ELIZABETH VON ARNIM
A funny and accomplished novel by the author of *Elizabeth and Her German Garden* **£5.99**

£4.99

£2.99

£5.99

AVAILABILITY

All books are available from your local bookshop or direct from
Littlehampton Book Services Cash Sales, 14 Eldon Way, LinesideEstate, Littlehampton, West Sussex BN17 7HE. PRICES ARE SUBJECT TO CHANGE.

To order any of the books, please enclose a cheque (in £ sterling) made payable to Littlehampton Book Services, or phone your order through with credit card details (Access, Visa or Mastercard) on 0903 721596 (24 hour answering service) stating card number and expiry date. Please add £1.25 for package and postage to the total value of your order.

POETRY
IN EVERYMAN

A SELECTION

Silver Poets of the Sixteenth Century

EDITED BY
DOUGLAS BROOKS-DAVIES
A new edition of this famous
Everyman collection **£6.99**

Complete Poems

JOHN DONNE
The father of metaphysical verse in
this highly-acclaimed edition **£4.99**

Complete English Poems, Of Education, Areopagitica

JOHN MILTON
An excellent introduction to
Milton's poetry and prose **£6.99**

Selected Poems

JOHN DRYDEN
A poet's portrait of Restoration
England **£4.99**

Selected Poems

PERCY BYSSHE SHELLEY
'The essential Shelley' in one
volume **£3.50**

Women Romantic Poets 1780-1830: An Anthology

Hidden talent from the Romantic era,
rediscovered for the first time **£5.99**

Poems in Scots and English

ROBERT BURNS
The best of Scotland's greatest lyric
poet **£4.99**

Selected Poems

D. H. LAWRENCE
A newly-edited selection spanning
the whole of Lawrence's literary
career **£4.99**

The Poems

W. B. YEATS
Ireland's greatest lyric poet
surveyed in this ground-breaking
edition **£6.50**

£5.99

£4.99

£3.50
